# Core Music Theory
## for String Players

# Violin, Level 2

## Celine Gietzen

www.coremusictheory.com

*a comprehensive introduction to musical notation, harmony, terminology, and ear training*

*available for violin, viola, cello, and bass in eleven levels*

**Core Music Theory for String Players, Violin Level 2**, by Celine Gietzen
Copyright © 2015 by Celine Gietzen.  All rights reserved.
No part of this book may be reproduced or transmitted in any form or by any electronic or mechanical means
including information storage and retrieval systems, without written permission from the publisher.
ISBN  978-1-942638-06-3
www.coremusictheory.com

# FOR THE STUDENT

Making music is a joyous experience that enhances our lives like no other.  People of all cultures have been traveling this path for thousands of years.  Increasing your knowledge about music theory will make the study of music a richer experience for you.

Music theory will help you make sense of what you see on the printed page.  This knowledge will ultimately facilitate your interpretation of music and enable you to find your own personal style that you use to express yourself through music.  You're on a worthwhile journey!

Always use pencil when writing in this workbook.  Take your time, and follow the instructions carefully.  Have fun!

# FOR THE TEACHER

Core Music Theory for String Players is a comprehensive music theory program, designed to help string players understand music notation and to introduce basic harmony.  The series includes 11 volumes each for violin, viola, cello, and bass (Preparatory Level through Level 10).  One answer key is also available for each instrument, which includes all levels.

Every workbook contains review of previous levels.  While it is most beneficial for the student to complete every level of this series, it can be started at any level.  Children under the age of nine will benefit from parental guidance.  Students will likely require input from their teacher at the more advanced levels.

The workbooks are valuable for all music students.  They can also be used to prepare those students enrolled in the Music Teachers' Association of California's Certificate of Merit™ program.

{ "Certificate of Merit™" is an evaluation program of the Music Teachers' Association of California. }
{ Reference to "Certificate of Merit™" or "CM" does not imply that MTAC endorses this product. }

To order, visit www.coremusictheory.com.

## ART CREDITS

Front cover:  Angel_1978/istockphoto.com
Instrument & Bow:  lhfgraphics/istockphoto.com
Unit pages and back cover art:  Shutterstock Inc./P. I. Lart
Congratulations page:  Music Notes Vector by dragonartz.net

# TABLE OF CONTENTS

# Unit 1

We'll start by learning the names of the parts
of this beautiful instrument and bow. When you know what the
different parts are, you can understand what they do.
It's exciting to learn about how sound is generated,
to unravel the mystery.

Did you know that the first violin
was made over 500 years ago?
That's just about the time Columbus sailed to America!

Next, we'll look at the written music
and discuss what it all means. Those lines and dots
of music notation are a new language. You'll find
that you'll soon be fluent in this language.
It's known to people all over the world.

# Chapter 1
# THE INSTRUMENT

## Fingerings

The **open strings** (E, A, D, G from highest to lowest) are played with no left hand fingers down.
**1st position** is the normal placement of the left hand, with 1st finger one note above the open string.
Each finger of the left hand is assigned a number.

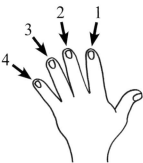

## Bowings

A **bowing** is a symbol that indicates which direction to move the bow.

| | | |
|---|---|---|
| ⊓ | **down bow** | move the bow toward the tip |
| V | **up bow** | move the bow toward the frog |

**pizzicato** (*pizz.*): pluck the string
**arco**: play with the bow

1. Draw down bows and up bows below, following the example shown. To draw a down bow, start in the upper left corner and then go down, up, right, and down.

⊓ ☐ ☐ ☐ ☐    V ☐ ☐ ☐ ☐

## Sound

**Sound** is vibration which travels through the air to reach our ears. **Rosin**, made from pine tree resin, enables the bow hair to grip the string to make it vibrate. Have you ever used a bow with absolutely no rosin? There is no sound!

Play an open string pizzicato, then arco. The vibrations travel through the bridge and the sound post. They bounce around inside where they are **amplified** (they become stronger and louder). They come out through the f-holes and through the entire body of the instrument.

This amplification is so powerful that the sound of one violin can fill an entire concert hall. It can project over a full symphony orchestra.

Study all of these parts of the instrument and bow.

# Violin

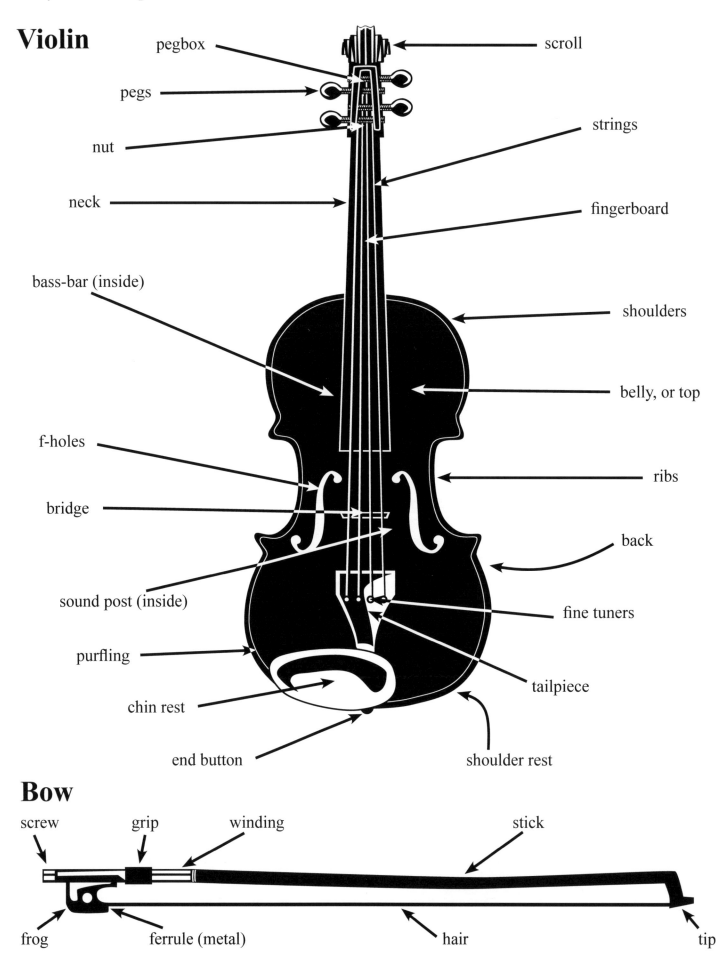

pegbox

pegs

nut

neck

scroll

strings

fingerboard

bass-bar (inside)

shoulders

belly, or top

f-holes

bridge

ribs

back

sound post (inside)

fine tuners

purfling

chin rest

end button

tailpiece

shoulder rest

# Bow

screw

grip

winding

stick

frog

ferrule (metal)

hair

tip

# *Going Beyond*

A **composer** is a person who writes music.
A **luthier** (LOO-thee-ur) is a person who makes and repairs stringed instruments.
The family of bowed stringed instruments includes the violin, viola, cello, and bass.
A musical composition for violin is a "piece" (not a "song," which is written for a singer).

2. Why do string players use rosin? (Check one.)

_____ a) To make the bow hair smooth so it can glide

_____ b) To add beauty to the instrument

_____ c) To help the bow grip the string

_____ d) To keep the bow hair clean

3. Write the term that means "play with the bow." _____

4. What is the finger number for the left hand middle finger? _____

5. A person who writes music is called a luthier.   True  /  False

6. What is the note name of the lowest string on the violin? _____

7. What is the finger number for the left hand little finger? _____

8. The string must vibrate to create sound.   True  /  False

9. What do you call a person who repairs cellos? _____

10. In the box to the right, write the bowing ( ⊓ or ∨ ) that fits each description below.

   a. Start near the frog and move toward the frog.

   b. Start at the frog and move toward the tip.

   c. Start in the middle and move toward the frog.

   d. Start in the middle and move toward the tip.

11. Sound is:  a) heat,  b) vibration,  c) gravity,  d) electricity  _____

12. Write the term that means "pluck the string." _____

13.  The bowed string instrument family includes the following 4 instruments:

_____   _____   _____   _____

14. To amplify means to make:  a) higher,   b) brighter,  c) darker,  d) louder  _____

# Chapter 2
# THE STAFF

Music is written on a group of 5 lines and 4 spaces, called the **staff**. You can remember this by thinking of your hand—you have 5 fingers and 4 spaces in between them. For more than one staff we say **staves** (not "staffs"). The lines and spaces are numbered from the bottom to the top.

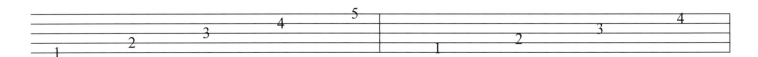

**Notes** are symbols used to write music. Notes that sound high are placed on the higher lines and spaces, while the lower sounding notes go on the lower lines and spaces. When more room is needed to go higher or lower than the staff allows, lines are added. These are called **leger lines** (also spelled "ledger lines").

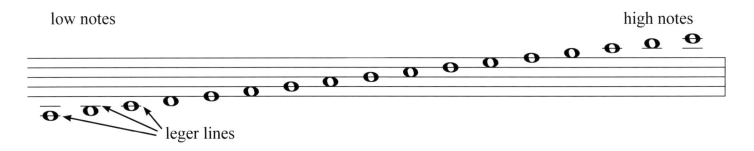

low notes                                                                 high notes

leger lines

Vertical lines called **bar lines** are written on the staff to separate the music into small sections. Each section is called a **measure** or a **bar**. Every measure is assigned a number. **Measure numbers** are often found at the beginning of each line of music (each new staff). At the end of a piece of music, a **double bar** (also called a double bar line) is placed to indicate the end.

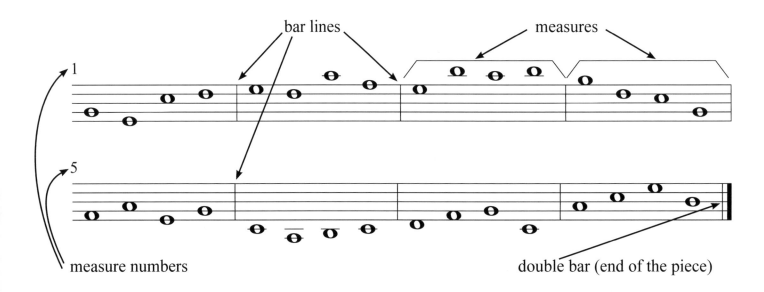

bar lines                                    measures

measure numbers                              double bar (end of the piece)

A **repeat sign** is a double bar with two dots. This sign tells the musician to go back and play the music again. After repeating, go to the next measure after the repeat sign and continue playing.

Sometimes a repeat sign leads back to another repeat with the dots to the right of the double bar (referred to as a forward repeat). If there is no forward repeat sign to return to, go back to the beginning of the piece.

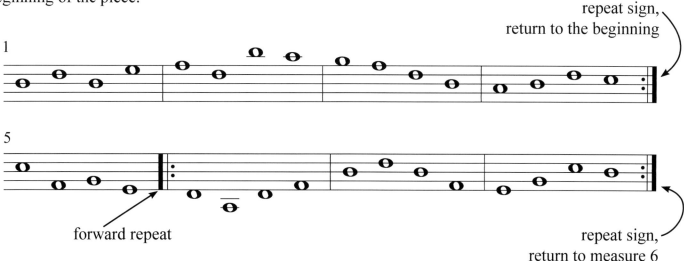

1. Answer the following questions about the musical example above.

    a. Which measure has the most low notes? _____

    b. Which 2 measures have leger line notes? _____ and _____

    c. What is the measure number of the 3rd measure of the 2nd line? _____

    d. What is the measure number of the last measure of the 1st line? _____

2. A repeat sign sometimes means to repeat back to another repeat sign.   True  /  False

3. The top staff line is referred to as the 1st line.   True  /  False

4. What is used to divide the music into measures? _____

5. ✪  What do you call the line that is drawn through this note? _____

6. What indicates that you have reached the end of the music? _____

A **1st ending** and **2nd ending** is another way music can repeat. Play through to the end of the 1st ending (it ends with a repeat sign). On the second time through (after the repeat), skip over the 1st ending.

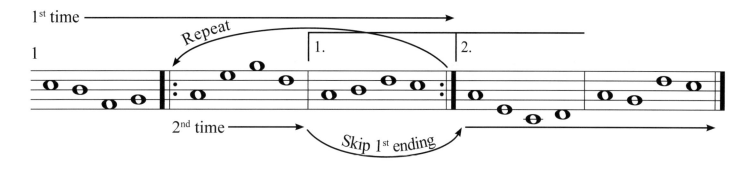

**Italian** words can also be used to indicate repeats. Most musical terms (such as *pizzicato* and *arco*) are Italian. Memorize the terms **D.C. al Fine** and **D.S. al Fine** (below). D.C. stands for "*da capo*" which means "from the head" (go back to the beginning). D.S., or "*dal segno,*" means "from the sign." After a D.C. or D.S., skip all repeats.

| | | |
|---|---|---|
| *Fine* | (FEE nay) | end (remember, it's like "finish") |
| *D.C. al Fine* | | return to the beginning, then end at the *Fine* |
| *D.S. al Fine* | | return to the sign 𝄋, then end at the *Fine* |

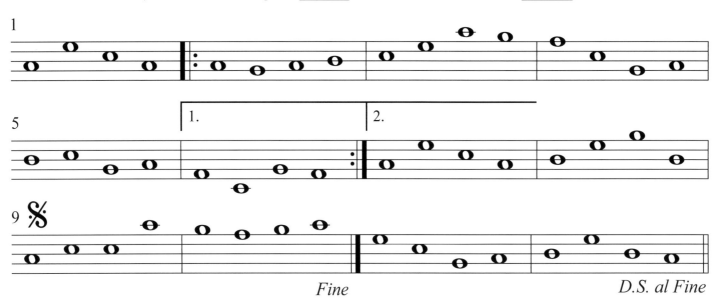

Answer the following questions about the musical example above.

Which measure is played after...
1. measure 6 (the 1ˢᵗ time through)? _____
2. measure 8? _____
3. measure 2 (the 2ⁿᵈ time through)? _____

How many times do you play...
4. measure 2? _____
5. measure 6? _____
6. measure 7? _____

Answer the following questions about the musical example above.

Which measure is played after...
7. measure 6? _____
8. measure 12? _____
9. measure 1? _____
10. measure 5 (the 1ˢᵗ time through)? _____
11. measure 10 (the 1ˢᵗ time through)? _____

How many times do you play...
12. measure 1? _____
13. measure 2? _____
14. measure 6? _____
15. measure 9? _____
16. measure 11? _____

# Chapter 3
# NOTE VALUES

Music is generally played with a steady beat. Some notes are played very quickly, while others last for several **counts**, or **beats**. A **note value** is the length of the note; it indicates how many counts to hold each note.

A **quarter note** is the note that often receives one beat. It has a black **notehead** and a **stem**.

Quarter notes:

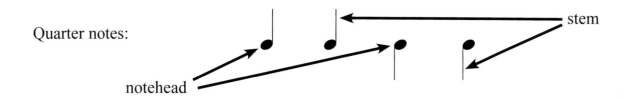

When notes are low on the staff (below the middle line), the stems go up. Notes above the middle line are written with down stems. This ensures that the notes fit well onto the staff. Notes on the middle line can have a stem going either direction.

Notice that the **up stems** are on the right side of the notehead, while the **down stems** are on the left side of the note.

1. On the staff below, add a stem to each notehead to form quarter notes. Remember to choose an up or a down stem based upon how high or low the note is, and put the stem on the correct side of the notehead (up on the right and down on the left).

2. On the staff below, circle the notes with incorrect stems.

The quarter note typically lasts for one beat.  There are many other kinds of notes that are longer (slower) or shorter (faster).

The **half note, dotted half note,** and **whole note** are all longer (slower) than the quarter note.  The half note is held for 2 beats, the dotted half note for 3 beats, and the whole note is held for 4 beats.

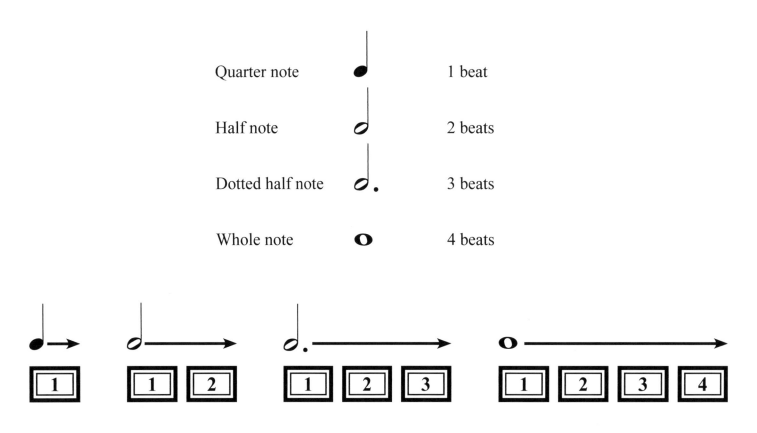

To draw a quarter note, first draw an oval for the notehead, then fill it in.  Without lifting your pencil from the paper, draw the stem (starting at the notehead).  To draw a half note, first draw an oval, then draw the stem starting from the notehead.  The whole note is a simple oval.  Do not fill in the sides for half notes and whole notes as you see in printed music.  To draw a leger line note, first draw the leger lines, then draw the notehead.

3.  Draw the notes below, following the example shown.

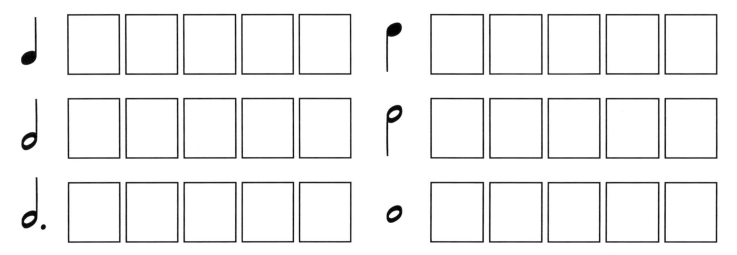

The **eighth note** is shorter (faster) than the quarter note. Eighth notes can be written two different ways: with **flags** attached to the stem, or with **beams** connecting them together. The eighth note is held for ½ of a beat; it takes two eighth notes to make one full beat.

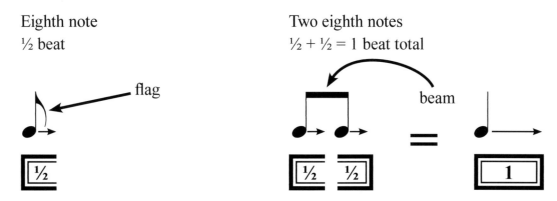

To a draw a single eighth note, first draw the notehead, then (without lifting your pencil off of the paper) draw the stem, and finally the flag. Notice that single eighth notes have the flag on the right side of the stem whether the stem is going up or down. For beamed eighths, draw the noteheads, then the stems (starting from the notehead), and finally connect the stems together.

4. Draw eighth notes below, following the example shown.

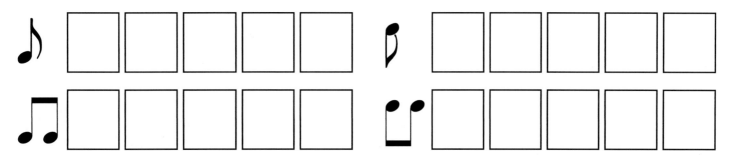

The **sixteenth note** is twice as fast as the eighth note. There are two eighth notes in a beat (in a quarter note), and there are four sixteenth notes in a quarter note beat. To draw a sixteenth note, first draw an eighth note, and then add an extra flag or beam (closer to the notehead than the first one you drew). Connect the ends of the flags to one another.

Sixteenth notes:

5. Draw sixteenth notes below, following the example shown.

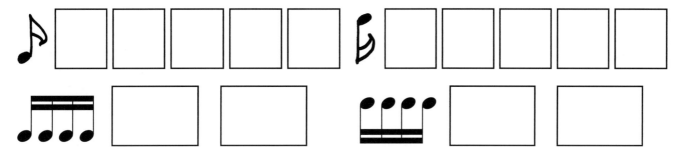

A **rest** is written in the music to indicate silence. Like notes, rests are also held for different lengths. They have the same name as the notes of the same value. (Note: the whole rest isn't always exactly 4 beats! It lasts for a whole measure.)

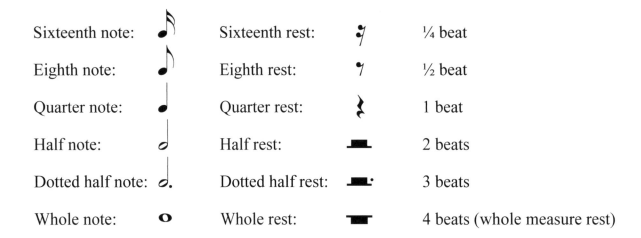

| | | | |
|---|---|---|---|
| Sixteenth note: ♬ | Sixteenth rest: | | ¼ beat |
| Eighth note: ♪ | Eighth rest: | | ½ beat |
| Quarter note: ♩ | Quarter rest: | | 1 beat |
| Half note: 𝅗𝅥 | Half rest: | | 2 beats |
| Dotted half note: 𝅗𝅥. | Dotted half rest: | | 3 beats |
| Whole note: 𝅝 | Whole rest: | | 4 beats (whole measure rest) |

6. Draw quarter, eighth, and sixteenth rests below, following the example shown. To draw a quarter rest, first make a Z (at an angle), then a C below it. Trace the sample quarter rest below several times before writing your own. The eighth rest is made by drawing a heavy dot, then a 7 with a slightly curved top. To make a sixteenth rest, first draw an eighth rest, then add an extra flag.

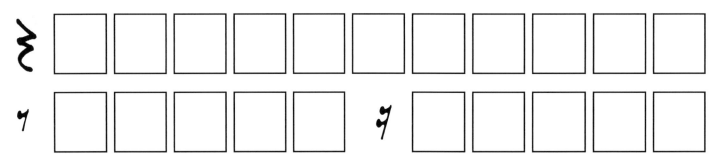

Half rests, dotted half rests, and whole rests are all written in the 3rd space. They look similar, but half rests and dotted half rests are written above the line and whole rests are written below it. To remember the difference between them, think of the half rest as a hat and the whole rest as a hole.

A half rest looks like a hat.

A whole rest looks like a hole.

7. Draw 6 half rests and 6 whole rests below, following the example shown. Be precise in your writing so the rest does not fill the entire 3rd space.

# UNIT 1 REVIEW

## The Instrument

Finger numbers:  1, 2, 3, 4

Open strings:  E, A, D, G (from highest to lowest)

1st position:  Placing the left hand with 1st finger one note above the open string

⊓ Down bow:  Move the bow toward the tip

∨ Up bow:  Move the bow toward the frog

*pizz.* Pizzicato:  Pluck the string

*arco* Play with the bow

## The Staff

Staff:  The group of 5 lines and 4 spaces where the music is written

The lines and spaces on the staff are numbered from the bottom to the top

High notes are closer to the top of the staff, and low notes are closer to the bottom

Bar lines:  Lines on the staff that separate the music into small sections

Measure:  The area between bar lines

Bar:  Another word for measure

‖ Double bar:  The end of the music

:‖ Repeat sign:  Go back and play the music again

1st and 2nd ending:  Play the 1st ending; repeat; skip the 1st ending the second time through

*D.C. al Fine (Da Capo al Fine):*  Return to the beginning, then end at the *Fine*

*D.S. al Fine (Dal Segno al Fine):*  Return to the sign 𝄋, then end at the *Fine*

## Note Values

Note value:  The length of a note; how many counts to hold each note

♪ 𝄿 Sixteenth note & rest:  The note or rest that receives ¼ of a beat (4 in a beat)

♪ 𝄾 Eighth note & rest:  The note or rest that receives ½ of a beat (2 in a beat)

♩ 𝄽 Quarter note & rest:  The note or rest that receives one beat

𝅗𝅥 ▬ Half note & rest:  The note or rest that receives two beats

𝅗𝅥. ▬· Dotted half note & rest:  The note or rest that receives three beats

𝅝 Whole note:  The note that receives four beats

▬ Whole rest:  The rest that lasts for an entire measure

Notehead:  The main round part of a note

Stem:  The line coming away from a notehead

Lower notes have up stems, and higher notes have down stems

Up stems are on the right side of the notehead, and down stems are on the left side

1. Never play from the 1ˢᵗ ending directly to the 2ⁿᵈ ending.   True  /  False

2. Write the word used in music that means "the end." _____

3. Up stems always go on the right side of the notehead.   True  /  False

4. Write the bow marking that means to play from the middle to the tip. ☐

5. How many beats are in a dotted half note? _____

6. What is the name of the highest string on the violin? _____

7. Musical terms are mostly written in French.   True  /  False

8. A note on the 4ᵗʰ space is higher than a note on the 1ˢᵗ line.   True  /  False

9. What is another word for **measure**? _____

10. Write a repeat sign. ☐

11. How many sixteenth notes are in a quarter note? _____

12. Write the musical term that means to play with the bow. _____

13. What is the finger number for the left hand middle finger? _____

14. *Fine* means go back to the beginning and play again.   True  /  False

15. What is the number of the bottom space of the staff? _____

16. *D.S. al Fine* means repeat back to the beginning, then end at the *Fine*.   True  /  False

17. Draw the note that is held for ½ of one beat. ☐

18. When you see *pizz.* in the music, you should play with the bow.   True  /  False

19. Draw the rest that lasts for one beat. ☐

20. The sixteenth note flag always goes on the right side of the stem.   True  /  False

21. For how many counts is a half note held? _____

22. The whole rest sits on top of the 3ʳᵈ line.   True  /  False

23. What is the name of the sign that indicates the end of the piece? _____

24. Identify the notes and rests on the staff below, following the example shown.

|  | a. | b. | c. | d. | e. | f. | g. | h. | i. |

quarter _____ _____ _____ _____ _____ _____ _____ _____ _____

note _____ _____ _____ _____ _____ _____ _____ _____ _____

# Unit 2

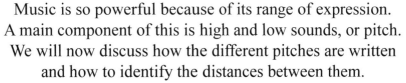

Music is so powerful because of its range of expression.
A main component of this is high and low sounds, or pitch.
We will now discuss how the different pitches are written
and how to identify the distances between them.

We'll learn about the piano keyboard, and figure out how
that can help you find your way around the notes on the violin.
The piano is a great way to learn about notes
because it's so clearly organized, like a road map.
Once you understand the map, you will be able to
navigate your way around the notes on the violin with ease.

# Chapter 4
# PITCH

The **pitch** of a sound refers to how high or low it is. There are 7 letters in the **musical alphabet**: A, B, C, D, E, F, and G. The notes get higher in pitch from A to G. Because there are more than 7 possible sounds (sounds that are even higher or lower), the letters repeat.

As you move up from a line to a space on the staff, the note names move up in alphabetical order. The **clef** is a sign at the beginning of the music that indicates where a certain pitch is. Violinists read music in **treble clef**. The treble clef is called the **G clef** because it has a spiral that curls around the line for the note G.

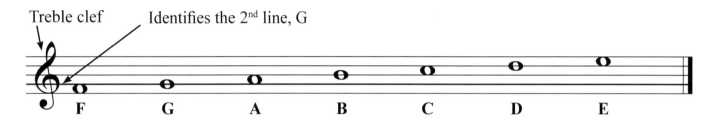

When drawing the treble clef, it is important to curl the center of the spiral around the correct line. Otherwise the G line is not properly indicated.

1. Draw 10 treble clefs on the staff below. Start at the bottom, and be sure to place the spiral correctly. Trace the printed treble clef several times before drawing your own.

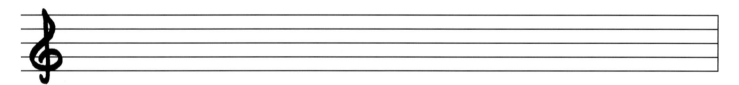

The **open strings** are easy to find on the staff. The highest string (open E) is the top space. The open A is on the second space, the open D is just below the bottom line, and the lowest string (open G) is under the second leger line below the staff.

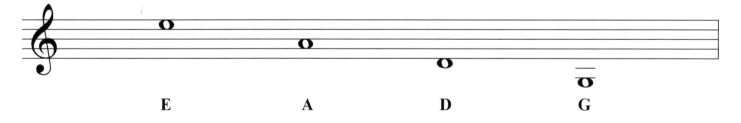

2. Draw a treble clef. Using quarter notes, write the open string notes on the staff below.

Every musician needs to be familiar with the piano keyboard. The notes get higher to the right and lower to the left. Each white key is named after a different letter of the musical alphabet. The black keys are grouped in sets of two and three. To find the note C, look just to the left of any group of two black keys.

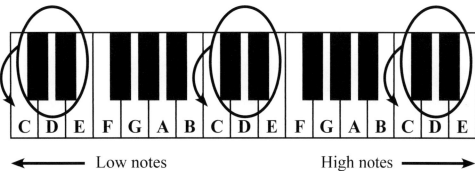

◄——— Low notes        High notes ———►

3. Write all of the F's on the keyboard below.

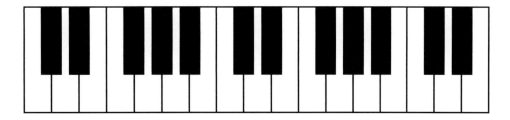

Here are all of the notes you need to know, from open G to the B above the staff.

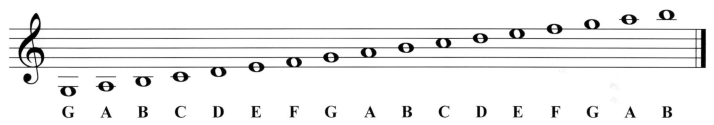

G  A  B  C  D  E  F  G  A  B  C  D  E  F  G  A  B

To read music, you'll need to identify the note names very quickly. The treble clef line notes are E, G, B, D, and F. The space notes are F, A, C, and E. In order to remember all of these notes, it is helpful to memorize the sentence "Every Good Bird Does Fly" for the line notes and the word "FACE" for the spaces.

Treble Clef Line Notes

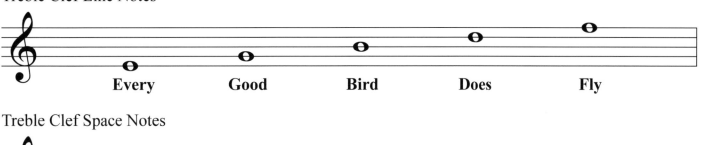

**Every**        **Good**        **Bird**        **Does**        **Fly**

Treble Clef Space Notes

F        A        C        E

Use this process to name a note: 1) Is it on a line or a space? 2) Should you use the sentence "Every Good Bird Does Fly" or the word FACE? 3) Using the words of your sentence (or letters of the word FACE), count up from the bottom of the staff.

Example:

1) Is it on a line or a space? It is a space note.
2) Which sentence or word applies?
   Space note word: "FACE"
3) Count the spaces from the bottom up:
   F, A, **C**, E. It's "C" from the word "FACE."

4. Write the note name under each note on the staff below.

_____  _____  _____  _____  _____  _____  _____  _____  _____  _____

If a note is on a leger line, count from line to space alphabetically to find the note name. Study the leger line notes below carefully. Memorize these note names.

5. Write the note name under each note on the staves below.

When writing a note on the staff, make the notehead small enough so that it is placed precisely within the space or on the line. Be clear in your note writing to avoid confusion.

6. Circle the 5 notes that are written incorrectly on the staff below. The correctly written notes are centered exactly on a line or in a space.

---

## Special Assignment

Making flashcards will help you identify notes on the staff quickly.

---

**SUPPLIES**: 17 index cards, ruler, pencil

Using the ruler, draw 5 lines on an index card to form a staff.
Draw the treble clef and one of the notes below.
On the back of the card, write the letter name.

---

Make a separate card for each of the notes below.
Show these flashcards to your teacher to be sure they have been done correctly.

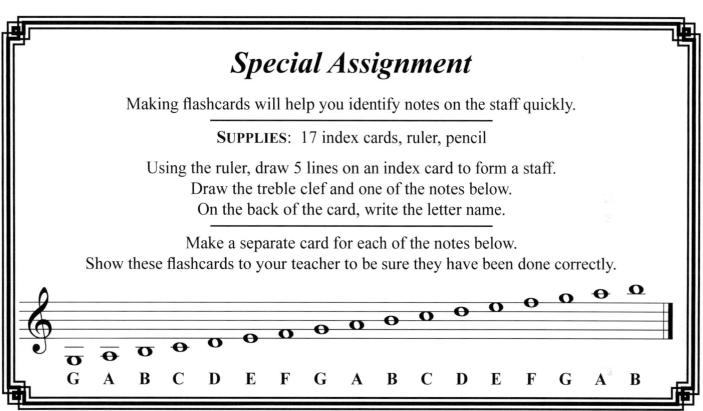

G A B C D E F G A B C D E F G A B

---

7. Draw a treble clef. Using <u>single sixteenth notes</u>, draw the notes below. (Follow the letter names below the staff.) Make all of your notes low notes, <u>ON or BELOW the 1st space F</u> on the staff.

          F          A          D          E          G          B          C

8. Draw a treble clef. Using <u>single eighth notes</u>, draw the notes on the staff below. Make all of your notes high notes, <u>ON or ABOVE the 3rd space C</u> on the staff.

          A          C          F          E          B          G          D

# Chapter 5
# ACCIDENTALS

A **half step** is the closest distance between two notes.  On the piano, most of the keys go from white to black, alternating back and forth.  These are all half steps.  There are two exceptions to this, where two white keys lie side by side.  Those notes are <u>B to C</u>, and <u>E to F</u>.  In this case, the two white keys are a half step apart because there is no key in between them.

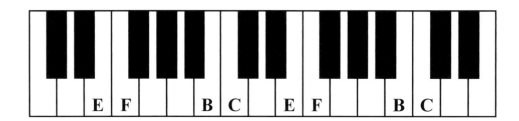

A **whole step** is the distance of two half steps.  Most of the white keys on the piano are a whole step apart, as are many of the black keys.  The keyboards below have half and whole steps marked.

## Half Steps

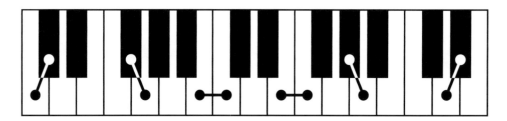

## Whole Steps

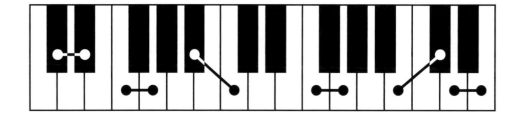

1.  Circle the key on the piano keyboard below that is a <u>whole step higher</u> than the key marked, following the example shown.

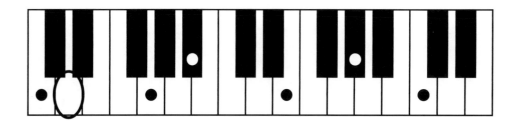

Half steps on the staff are marked with a ⌄ connecting the notes. This **half step mark** can be below the notes or above the notes (upside-down).

2. Mark all of the half steps on the musical example below, following the example shown. Remember there is a half step between <u>B to C</u> and <u>E to F</u>.

An **accidental** is a symbol that is placed before a note, which makes the note a half step higher or lower. There are three different accidentals: a **sharp** (makes the note higher), a **flat** (makes the note lower), and a **natural** (cancels out a sharp or a flat).

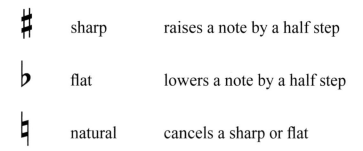

| ♯ | sharp | raises a note by a half step |
| ♭ | flat | lowers a note by a half step |
| ♮ | natural | cancels a sharp or flat |

To draw a sharp, simply make 4 lines like a number sign (don't thicken any of the lines as you see in printed music). The flat is a line then the right side of a heart. The natural sign is made by making an L, then a 7, and putting them together.

3. Draw sharps, flats, and naturals below, following the example shown.

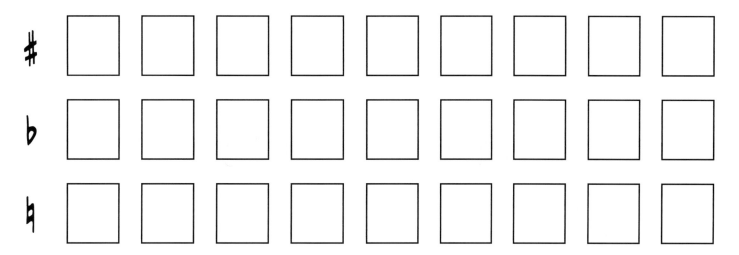

The natural notes are the white keys on the piano. To find a sharp, go one key to the right (a half step higher than the natural note).

Sharps on the piano are usually black keys, but for <u>B to C</u> and <u>E to F</u> it is another white key. This can be confusing because there are two names for these keys (F is also called E♯).

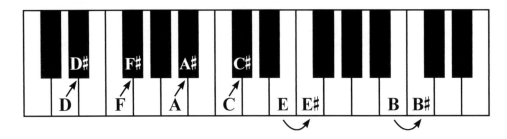

To find a flat on the piano, go one key to the left (a half step lower than the natural note).

As with the sharps, the flats on the piano are usually black keys, but in the case of <u>B to C</u> and <u>E to F</u> it is another white key.

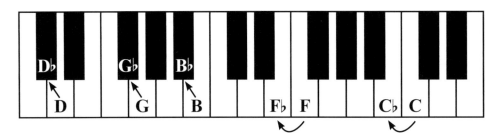

This means that each black key (and some white keys) have 2 different names. For example, the black key to the left of D is a half step lower, so that is called D♭. But that is the same key as the one to the right of C (a half step higher than C), and is therefore also called C♯.

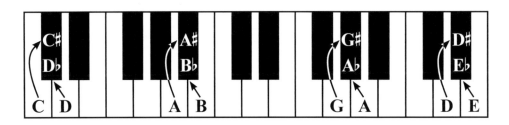

## Going Beyond

When there are two names for the same note in music, it is called an **enharmonic**.
A♯ is the enharmonic of B♭.   D♭ is the enharmonic of C♯.
What is the enharmonic of F♯?
What is the enharmonic of F♭?

Another way to think about the pattern of notes in the musical alphabet is to envision them as a set of stairs. Remember that the natural notes B to C and E to F are both just a half step apart, but all of the other notes are a whole step apart. Memorize these **natural note half steps** so you can easily find your way around your instrument.

Study the diagram below. Cover up part of the staircase and quiz yourself on what comes next.

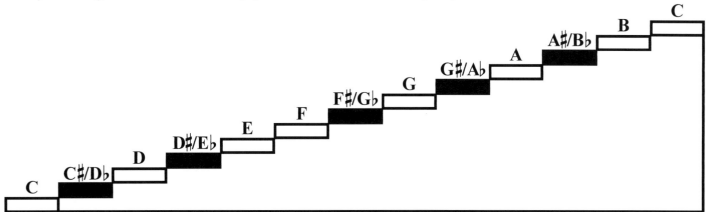

4. Write TWO names for each of the keys indicated on the piano keyboard below.

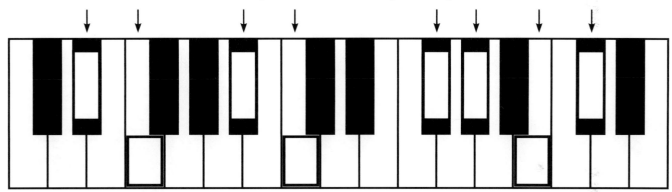

Writing accidentals on the staff is similar to writing notes. It is important that the center of the accidental is placed precisely and that it is not too large. When accidentals are written in the music, they always come before the note, but when we talk about notes or write letter names we say and write the accidental after the note. Study this example of accidentals written correctly.

5. Draw a treble clef. Next, draw single eighth notes on the staff below. (Follow the letter names below the staff.) Make all of your notes low notes, ON or BELOW the 1st space F.

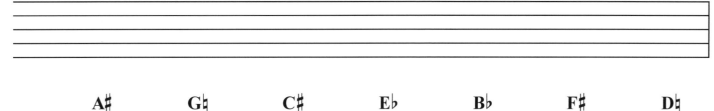

A♯          G♮          C♯          E♭          B♭          F♯          D♮

Accidentals last for an entire measure. In a new measure, the note is no longer sharp or flat; the bar line cancels it out. A natural sign also cancels a sharp or a flat. Study the example below.

A    C♯ E C♯    C    B    A♯    A  G♯ A  C♯ E  G♯  G  F♯    F    G♯    A

6. Write the note name under each note on the staff below. Do not use natural signs. Sharps and flats must have the sharp or flat sign included <u>after</u> the letter name of the note.

___ ___ ___ ___ ___ ___ ___ ___ ___ ___ ___ ___ ___ ___ ___ ___ ___ ___

7. Mark all of the half steps on the musical example below, following the example shown. Don't overlook notes that are separated by a bar line.

8. Write <u>H</u> for half step or <u>W</u> for whole step below, following the example shown.

W   ___  ___  ___  ___  ___  ___  ___  ___  ___  ___  ___  ___  ___  ___

9. Write one note in each measure, following the example shown. Use whole notes. You will need to use accidentals in some of your answers. Read the instructions below each measure carefully.

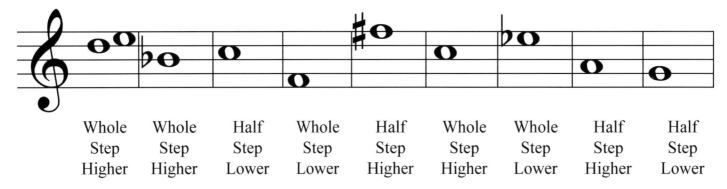

| Whole Step Higher | Whole Step Higher | Half Step Lower | Whole Step Lower | Half Step Higher | Whole Step Higher | Whole Step Lower | Half Step Higher | Half Step Lower |
|---|---|---|---|---|---|---|---|---|

# Chapter 6
# ON THE INSTRUMENT

## First Position

The fingering chart to the right and the staff below show the notes in 1st position.

Notice that the higher pitches are lower on the fingering chart; as you go down toward the bridge, the notes get higher. This can be confusing! Remember, going down the fingerboard (toward the bridge) the notes get higher, and going up (toward the scroll) the notes are lower.

In 1st position, 2nd finger is often placed close to 3rd finger. This is referred to as **high 2** and is indicated on the chart with an up arrow.

Memorize the whole steps and half steps in 1st position:
Open string to 1st finger is a whole step.
1st finger to high 2nd is a whole step.
2nd to 3rd finger is a half step.
3rd to 4th finger is a whole step.

Notice that 4th finger plays the same note as the next open string (except on the E string, because there is no higher string).

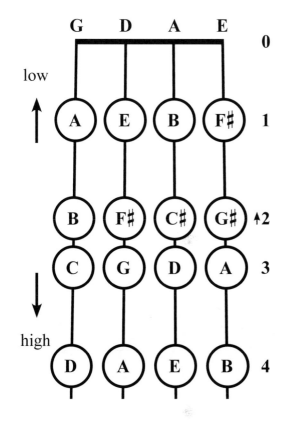

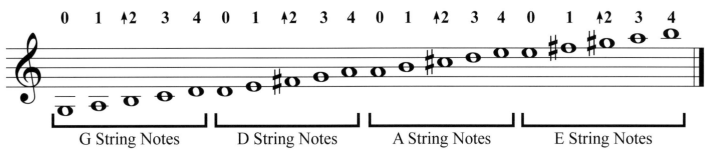

Use the diagram of the stairs below to help reinforce your knowledge of the notes on the lower strings.

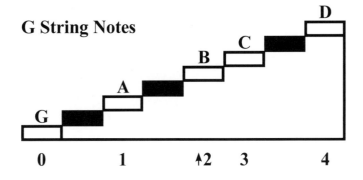

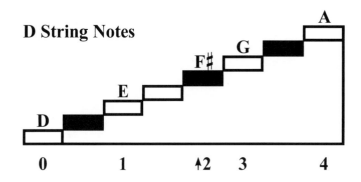

# Low 2

In 1st position, to play the note between 1st finger and high 2nd finger (G on the E string, for example), the 2nd finger is placed close to the 1st. We call that **low 2**. Even though it is higher on the fingering chart, it sounds lower, so low 2 is indicated with a down arrow. Remember that sharps and flats each have two names, and are sometimes named differently (B♭ is also A♯).

1. Write a finger number above each note in 1st position, following the example shown. Use arrows to indicate low 2 and high 2.

# Low 1

1st finger can also reach lower (closer to the nut). This is called **low 1**, and is indicated with a down arrow. On the fingering chart, only one note name is used for each note. But be aware that each note has two names. For example, low 1 on the D string can be called E♭ or D♯.

2. Write a finger number above each note in 1st position, following the example shown. Use arrows to indicate low 1, low 2, and high 2.

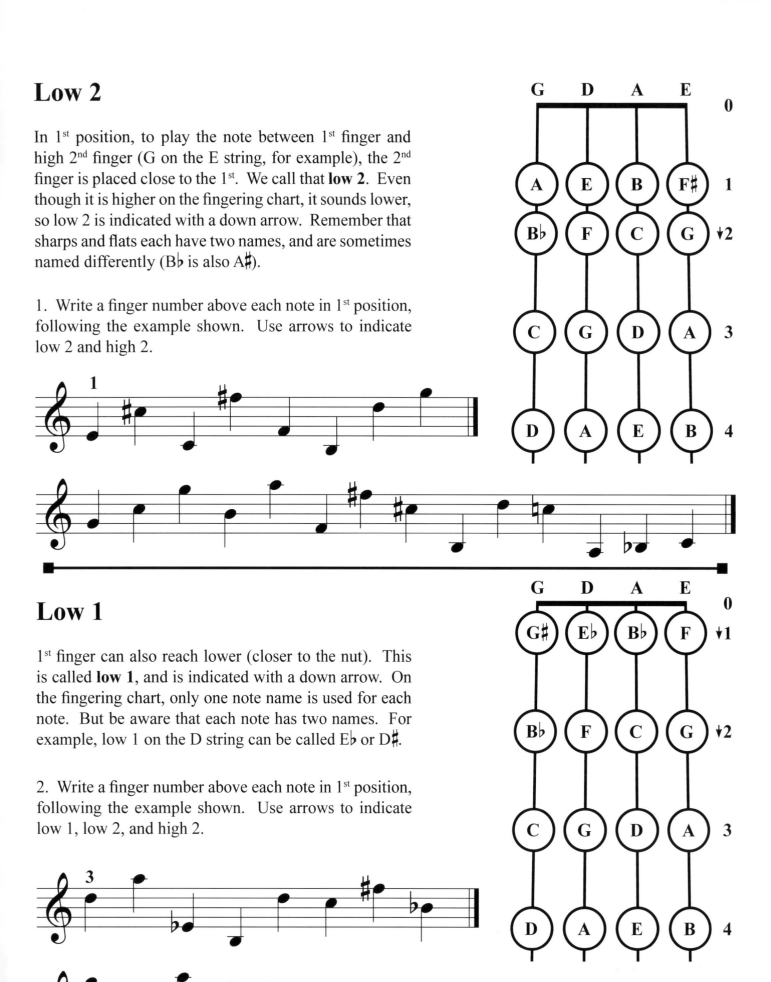

# High 3

To play the note between 3$^{rd}$ finger and 4$^{th}$ finger in 1$^{st}$ position, reach the 3$^{rd}$ finger closer to the 4$^{th}$. This is called **high 3**, and is indicated with an up arrow. Don't forget that each sharp or flat actually has two names, not only the one you see on the fingering chart.

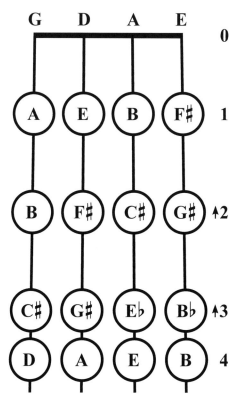

3. Write a finger number above each note in 1$^{st}$ position, following the example shown. Use arrows to indicate low 1, low 2, high 2, and high 3.

## Special Assignment

Making flashcards will help you identify notes on the instrument quickly.

Supplies: 28 index cards, pencil
On the front of the card, write a finger number and string name, for example "3 on A"
On the back of the card, write the letter name of the note, for example "D"

Make a separate card for each of the notes you've learned. You will have 7 cards for each string.
For example: ↓1 on A, 1 on A, ↓2 on A, ↑2 on A, 3 on A, ↑3 on A, and 4 on A.
Show these flashcards to your teacher to be sure they have been done correctly.

4.  Write a finger number above each note in 1st position, following the example shown.  Use arrows to indicate low 1, low 2, high 2, and high 3.  If a note can be played by either 4th finger or open string, use 4 for 4th finger, do not use 0 for open.

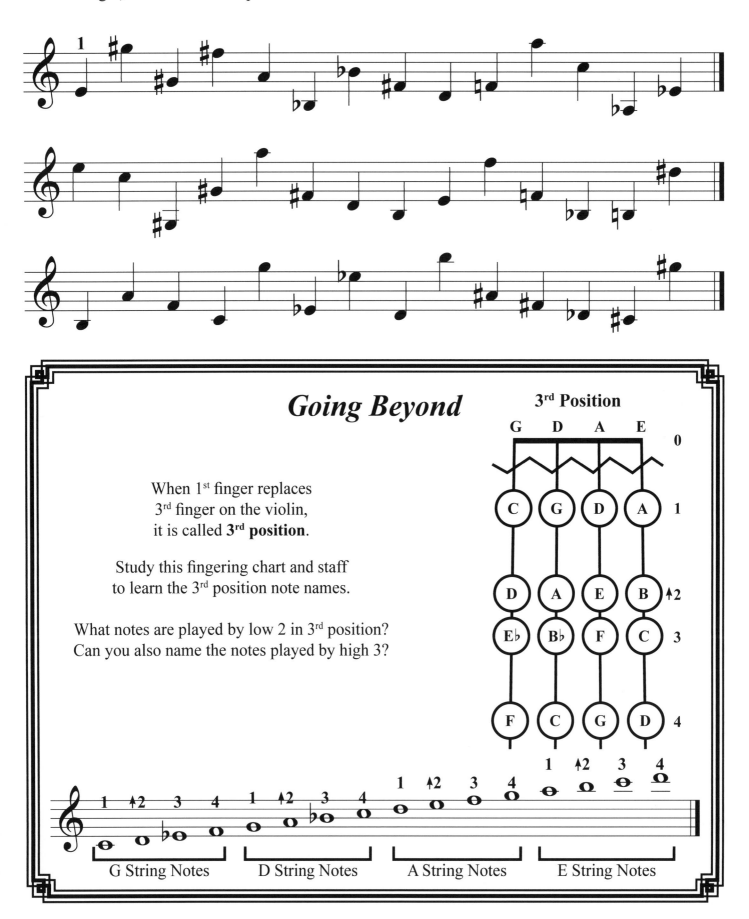

# Going Beyond

**3rd Position**

When 1st finger replaces 3rd finger on the violin, it is called **3rd position**.

Study this fingering chart and staff to learn the 3rd position note names.

What notes are played by low 2 in 3rd position? Can you also name the notes played by high 3?

# Articulations

An **articulation** is a symbol or word that gives detailed information about *how* to play the notes. Two basic articulations are **legato** (smoothly) and **staccato** (detached—short, separate notes, keeping the bow on the string). Like most musical terms, these words are Italian. If there is no other direction, play the notes legato.

Another articulation is **accent** which means play that note with emphasis, to grip the string with the bow for a strong attack. The word **fortepiano** means to start the note strongly and then immediately play softly. This term can also be called a **dynamic** marking, which is a word or symbol that tells the musician how loud or soft to play.

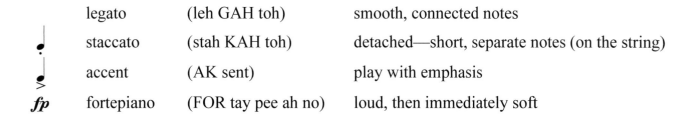

| | legato | (leh GAH toh) | smooth, connected notes |
| --- | --- | --- | --- |
| | staccato | (stah KAH toh) | detached—short, separate notes (on the string) |
| | accent | (AK sent) | play with emphasis |
| *fp* | fortepiano | (FOR tay pee ah no) | loud, then immediately soft |

---

## *Play It!*

Look for a piece you've played before that is intended to be played legato.
Play it staccato, then with accents, and finally with each note fortepiano.
Notice what a big difference this makes in the sound of the piece.

---

A curved line connecting two or more notes can be a **slur, tie**, or **detached slur**. A slur connects notes of different pitches and is played smoothly in one bow. A tie connects two notes of the same pitch and is held longer as if the notes are "tied" together. A detached slur (also called **hooked bow** or **slurred staccato**) has dots or dashes on the notes. It connects notes of different pitches *or* of the same pitch, and is played with a slight pause between the notes.

5. Write <u>S for slur</u>, <u>T for tie</u>, or <u>D for detached slur</u> below, following the examples shown.

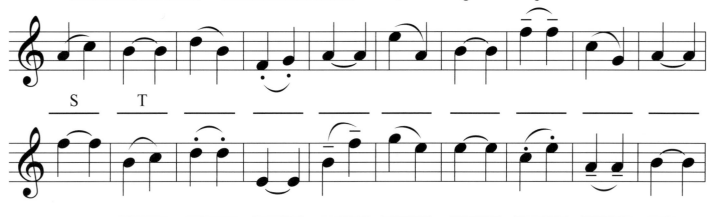

# UNIT 2 REVIEW

## Pitch

Pitch: A term which refers to how high or low a sound is

Musical alphabet: The 7 letters used to name notes, A B C D E F G

    Treble clef: The sign at the beginning of each line of music which identifies the note G

Notes on the staff and finger numbers in 1st position:

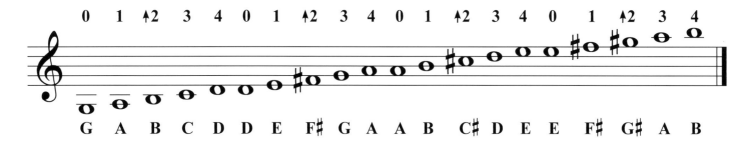

## Accidentals

Half step: The closest distance between two notes

Whole step: The distance of two half steps

Natural note half steps: <u>B to C</u> and <u>E to F</u> are the only natural notes that are a half step apart

Accidental: A symbol which makes a note one half step higher or lower for one measure

   ♯   Sharp sign: Raises a note by a half step

   ♭   Flat sign: Lowers a note by a half step

   ♮   Natural sign: Cancels out a sharp or a flat

## On the Instrument

High 2: 2nd finger is placed close to 3rd

Low 2: 2nd finger is placed close to 1st

Low 1: 1st finger is placed close to the nut

High 3: 3rd finger is placed close to 4th

Articulation: A symbol or word that indicates how to play a note

Legato: Smooth, connected notes with no pause between them

   Staccato: Short, separate notes; played on the string

   Accent: Play with emphasis

   *fp* Fortepiano: Loud, then immediately soft

   Slur: Connects two (or more) different notes in one bow

   Tie: Connects two notes of the same pitch; held as if the two notes were one

   Detached slur: A slur with a slight pause between notes

1. Tied notes are played slightly separated.   True   /   False

2. Draw the musical symbol which cancels out a sharp or flat.

3. The staff lines (starting at the top) are E, G, B, D, F.   True   /   False

4. The musical term which means to emphasize the note with a strong attack is _____.

5. Low 1 allows a violinist to reach notes a half step higher than the open string.   True   /   False

6. Detached slurs can also be called "hooked bows."   True   /   False

7. An articulation tells the musician how high or low to play a note.   True   /   False

8. Half steps are found between the natural notes B to C and _____ to _____.

9. Draw a treble clef.

10. Write a 1st position note name, following the example shown.

    a. 1st finger on the D string: ___E___

    b. 3rd finger on the A string: _____

    c. Low 2 on the G string: _____

    d. High 3 on the E string: _____

    e. 4th finger on the G string: _____

    f. Low 1 on the A string: _____

    g. 4th finger on the A string: _____

11. Write a 1st position finger number, following the example shown.

    a. E♭ on the D string: __↓1__

    b. G♯ on the D string: _____

    c. B♭ on the G string: _____

    d. B on the E string: _____

    e. F♯ on the D string: _____

    f. F on the E string: _____

    g. C♯ on the G string: _____

12. Write the finger number and the note name for each note in 1st position, following the example shown. Use arrows to indicate low 1, low 2, high 2, and high 3.

# Unit 3

Next we'll explore rhythm, the driving force of music.
Different rhythms can make us feel excited, in suspense,
or peaceful.  They can make us feel like dancing.  You'll learn how
to clap a rhythm and to count out loud while playing,
which will make you a leader in orchestras.

We'll go deeper into our study of pitch by learning
to identify steps and skips.  Being able to hear the difference
between these can help you learn how to play by ear.
You can use this skill to make up music on the spot
(to improvise) or to write music of your own (to compose).

Finally, we'll learn about scales and triads.
This is really exciting because scales and
triads are the building blocks of music!
Look at any piece of music, and you'll find scales.
If you know how to identify and play scales,
you'll play a new piece of music and it will seem familiar.
You'll feel like you've played it before.

# Chapter 7
# RHYTHM

**Rhythm** is the way note values are organized in time. Memorize the following note and rest values. The whole rest is the only exception to the chart below, it is not always worth 4 beats.

| | | | |
|---|---|---|---|
| Sixteenth note: ♬ | Sixteenth rest: | ¼ beat | |
| Eighth note: ♪ | Eighth rest: | ½ beat | |
| Quarter note: ♩ | Quarter rest: | 1 beat | |
| Half note: 𝅗𝅥 | Half rest: | 2 beats | |
| Dotted half note: 𝅗𝅥. | Dotted half rest: | 3 beats | |
| Whole note: 𝅝 | Whole rest: | 4 beats (whole measure rest) | |

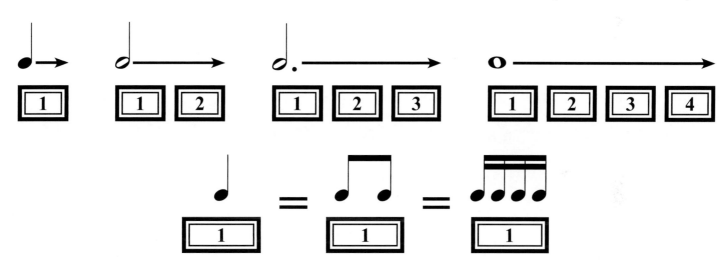

1. Write one <u>rest</u> in each box, following the example shown.

♪ + ♪ = [ 𝄽 ]     a. 𝄽 + ♫ = [ ]     b. ♬ = [ ]     c. + ♬ = [ ]

d. ♩ + 𝄽 = [ ]     e. + = [ ]     f. ♬ + ♬ = [ ]     g. ♩ + 𝅗𝅥. = [ ]

h. ♬ + = [ ]     i. 𝅗𝅥. + 𝄽 = [ ]     j. ♫ + 𝅗𝅥. = [ ]     k. + ♪ = [ ]

l. 𝄽 + 𝅗𝅥 = [ ]     m. 𝅗𝅥 + 𝅗𝅥 = [ ]     n. + = [ ]     o. 𝅗𝅥 + ♩ = [ ]

The numbers at the beginning of a piece are called the **time signature**. The **top number** tells the musician how many beats are in each measure. The first beat of each measure is the strongest.

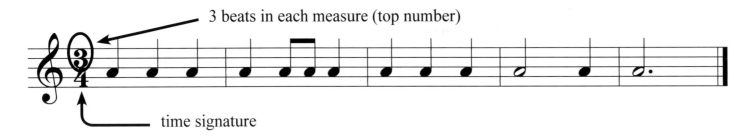

3 beats in each measure (top number)

time signature

The **bottom number** of the time signature indicates what kind of note gets one beat. This is often the number 4, which means the quarter note is held for one count. Think of this as the bottom number of a fraction; the fraction ¼ is a quarter.

**2** ← The number of beats in each measure (2)
**4** ← The kind of note that gets the beat (a quarter note)

Writing the beats into each measure will help you count accurately. When writing in the counts, be sure to write the number of each beat directly under the note or rest it applies to.

To count eighth notes, the word "and" is used in between the numbers. The "and" is written into the music as a plus sign. When eighth notes are present, count the "ands" or write in the plus signs for every measure of the piece. If there are no eighth notes, you don't need to use "ands" at all.

Line the counts up carefully. Always start a new measure with beat 1. Study the musical examples below to see how the counts are placed correctly.

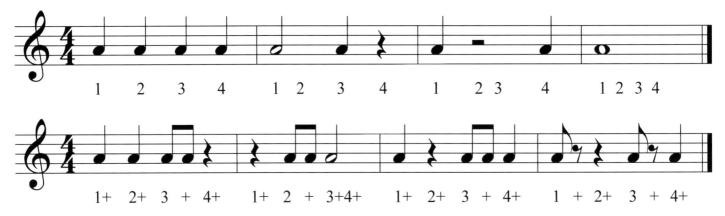

The whole rest is sometimes referred to as a **whole measure rest**, indicating that the length of the rest will change depending upon the time signature. Study the rests in the example below.

2. Write in the counts for the musical examples below. First check to see if there are eighth notes on the line, and if so use "ands" for every single beat. Place the counts carefully, directly under each beat.

There are four sixteenth notes in a quarter note beat. To count sixteenth notes, we say "1 ee and uh." This is written into the music as "1 e + a." Remember, first look to see which notes are in the line; if there is nothing shorter than a quarter note you don't need "ands" at all. If there are eighth notes, write "ands" throughout, and if there are sixteenths, write "e + a" after every single beat.

Study the musical example below. Notice how the counts are lined up under each note or rest.

1 e + a  2e +a 3e +a  1e +a  2  e + a  3e +a  1e + a 2 e +a  3e +a  1e+a 2 e +a 3e+a

3. Write in the counts for the musical examples below.

When asked to write bar lines into a musical example, first write in the counts. Then place the bar lines carefully so that they do not extend above or below the staff lines.

4. First write in the counts, then add bar lines to the musical examples below.

When learning a new piece of music it is valuable to clap and count the rhythms before playing. To do this, say the counts continuously, and clap when there is a note. Hold your hands together for the long notes, and open them apart on the rests. Count slowly and steadily, like the ticking of a clock.

In the example below, the X above a note means to clap on that beat. The line extending after it means hold your hands together (for the long notes). The O means move your hands apart (for a rest).

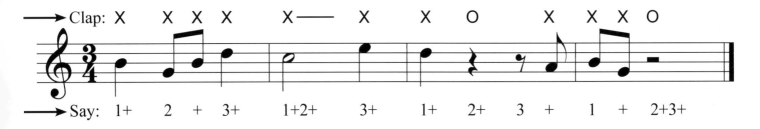

5. Practice clapping and counting each line of music on this page at a slow speed. Take this to your teacher to demonstrate how you clap and count.

The **tempo** is the speed of a piece of music. A **tempo marking** is often written just above the first bar of the music, and it can be changed later. This is usually an Italian word. For example, you may see the word **Allegro** which means fast and happily, or **Andante** which means a slow, walking tempo.

Other words and symbols are used to affect the tempo of the music.

| | | | |
|---|---|---|---|
| 𝄐 | **fermata** | (fur MAH tuh) | hold longer |
| *rit.* | **ritard** | (rih TARD) | gradually slower |
| *rit.* | **ritardando** | (rih tar DAHN doh) | gradually slower |
| *a tempo* | **a tempo** | (AH TEM poh) | return to the previous speed |

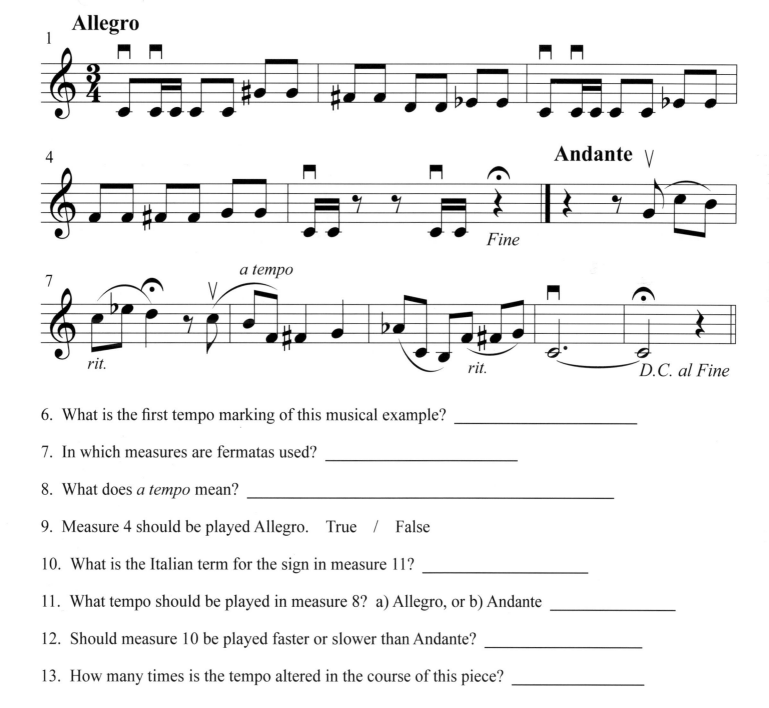

6. What is the first tempo marking of this musical example? _____

7. In which measures are fermatas used? _____

8. What does *a tempo* mean? _____

9. Measure 4 should be played Allegro.   True   /   False

10. What is the Italian term for the sign in measure 11? _____

11. What tempo should be played in measure 8?  a) Allegro, or b) Andante _____

12. Should measure 10 be played faster or slower than Andante? _____

13. How many times is the tempo altered in the course of this piece? _____

# Chapter 8
# INTERVALS

An **interval** is the distance between two notes.

When notes move by **step**, they go up or down on the staff from <u>line to space</u> or <u>space to line</u>. A step is called a **2nd** because two note names are used in order. This is not 2 half steps, just 2 letter names.

When notes **skip** they move from <u>line to line</u> or <u>space to space</u>. A skip is also called a **3rd**.

Notes that **repeat** stay on the same line or space. A repeat is also called a **unison**.

Accidentals do not affect 2nds and 3rds.

2nds (Steps)                                          3rds (Skips)

To determine the interval, count the letter names from the first note to the second one. In the first measure above, the notes go from F♯ to G; this distance of 2 note names (F, G) is a 2nd. In the fifth measure above, the notes go from A to C♯. This distance of 3 note names (A, B, C) is a 3rd.

1. Write <u>2nd</u>, <u>3rd</u>, or <u>unison</u> under each measure, following the example shown.

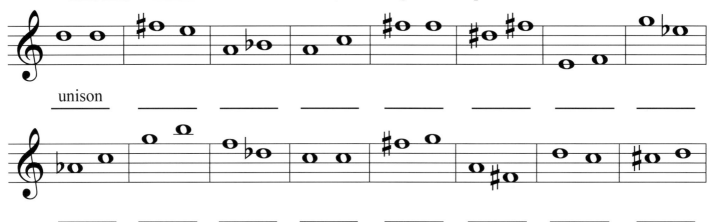

unison

2. Write one note in each measure, following the example shown. Use whole notes. Do not use accidentals in your answers.

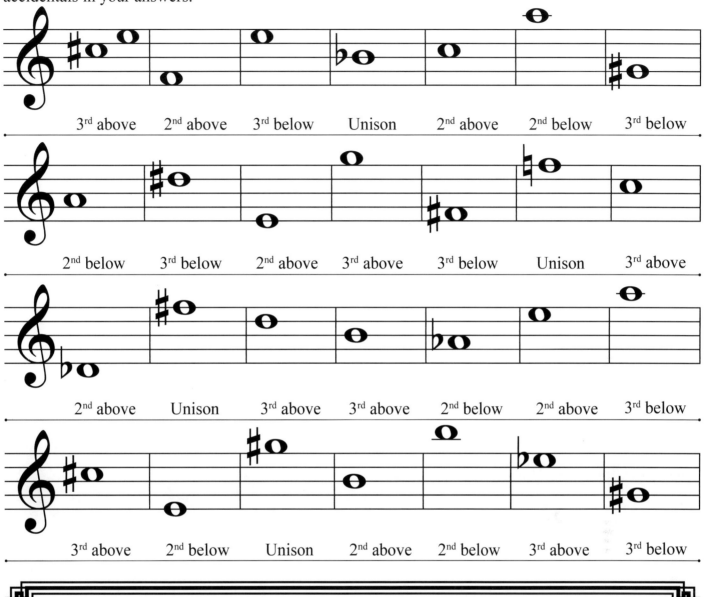

| 3rd above | 2nd above | 3rd below | Unison | 2nd above | 2nd below | 3rd below |

| 2nd below | 3rd below | 2nd above | 3rd above | 3rd below | Unison | 3rd above |

| 2nd above | Unison | 3rd above | 3rd above | 2nd below | 2nd above | 3rd below |

| 3rd above | 2nd below | Unison | 2nd above | 2nd below | 3rd above | 3rd below |

---

## Listen to Music

Ask your teacher to play either a 2nd or a 3rd.
Sing the interval to yourself. Tell your teacher which one you hear.
Do this repeatedly, until you can get the right answer every time.

---

On the violin, steps (2nds) are easy to find; simply go from one finger to the next. Sometimes the fingers will stretch (1st finger to high 2) and sometimes they are very close together (high 2 to 3rd finger), but they are still stepping. The reason for this is that a step can be either a half step or a whole step.

To play a skip (a 3rd), just skip over a finger (for example, 1st to 3rd finger). To play a skip across strings, go from 2nd finger to the next open string. That way, you are skipping just one note, the note played by the 3rd finger. You can play the same notes by using 2nd and 4th fingers. Remember, 4th finger plays the same note as the next open string.

Locate the notes (on the staff below) on the fingering chart (to the right). Notice how many different finger combinations can be used for 2nds or 3rds.

On the staff below, you will find just a few examples. Can you think of other finger combinations for 2nds and 3rds, not shown here?

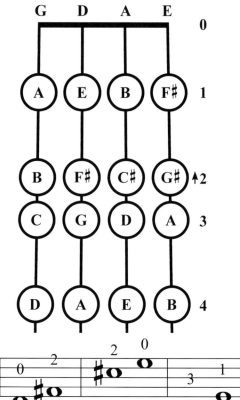

2nds (Steps)                                    3rds (Skips)

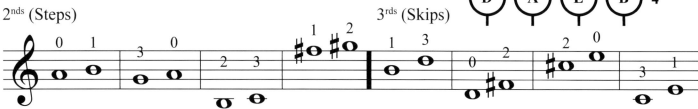

3. Start with the black note in each fingering chart below. Move up or down as directed, and shade in your answer. Follow the example below.

Example: 2nd lower    a. 3rd higher    b. 3rd lower    c. 3rd higher    d. 2nd lower

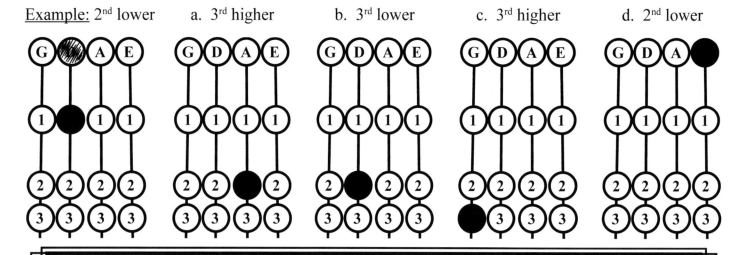

---

## Going Beyond

When it comes to intervals, 2nds and 3rds are only the beginning!
A 4th is 4 notes apart, a 5th is 5 notes apart, and so on.
The violin is tuned in 5ths. As we move from one string to the next string higher, we go up 5 letter names. If you count the letter names from D to A you'll count 5 letters (D, E, F, G, A).
Put any finger on the D string. Move that same finger over to the A string.
You've gone up a 5th!

# Chapter 9
# SCALES

A **scale** is a stepping pattern, made up of half steps and whole steps.  To build a scale, step up for 8 notes in a row.  Start and end on the same note name.

A **major scale** follows a specific pattern of half and whole steps.  There is always a half step between the 3rd and 4th notes, and also between the 7th and 8th notes.  All of the other intervals are whole steps.

The major scale pattern is:  <u>Whole, Whole, Half,    Whole, Whole, Whole, Half.</u>
Repeat this many times out loud, and commit it to memory.

The example below is a C Major Scale.  All natural notes are used (there are no sharps or flats).  The half step between the 3rd and 4th notes is from E to F, and the half step between the 7th and 8th notes is from B to C.  These are the natural note half steps.

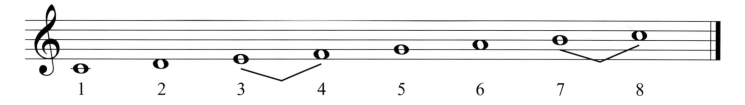

If the scale starts on a note other than C, sharps or flats need to be added so that the notes follow the major scale pattern.  Notice in the example below that the scale starts and ends on G.  The half step between the 3rd and 4th notes is from B to C, and between the 7th and 8th notes it is from F♯ to G.

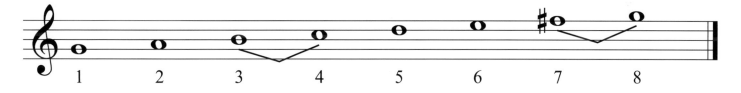

1. Add half step marks to the notes in the scales below.  Next, circle your answer on the right, to indicate whether or not the scale follows the major scale pattern.

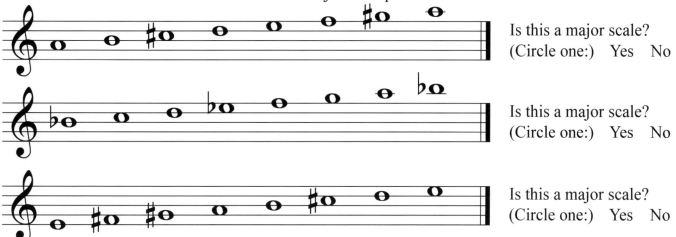

Is this a major scale?
(Circle one:)   Yes   No

Is this a major scale?
(Circle one:)   Yes   No

Is this a major scale?
(Circle one:)   Yes   No

Three common scales are C, G, and D. The C major scale has no sharps or flats, the G major scale has one sharp (F♯), and the D major scale has two sharps (F♯ and C♯). Memorize the sharps in these scales.

2. Add sharps (if necessary) to complete the major scales below.

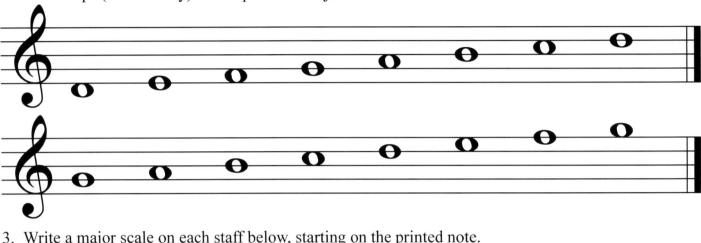

3. Write a major scale on each staff below, starting on the printed note.

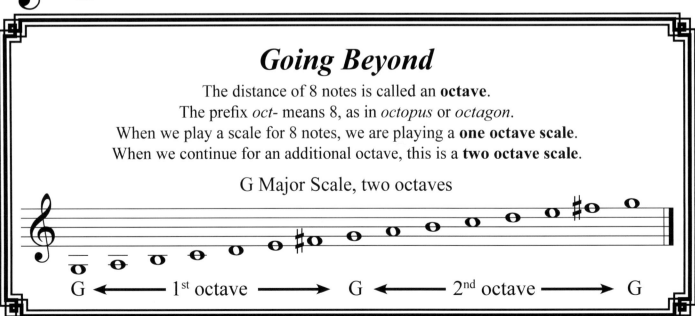

## Going Beyond

The distance of 8 notes is called an **octave**.
The prefix *oct-* means 8, as in *octopus* or *octagon*.
When we play a scale for 8 notes, we are playing a **one octave scale**.
When we continue for an additional octave, this is a **two octave scale**.

G Major Scale, two octaves

G ←——— 1st octave ———→ G ←——— 2nd octave ———→ G

# Chapter 10
# TRIADS

A **chord** is two or more notes played at the same time. It is easy to play chords on the piano or guitar, but violinists don't play them as often. It is easier for us to play one note at a time.

An **arpeggio** is a broken chord, meaning the notes are broken up and played one at a time. This is much easier to play on the violin.

A **triad** is a three-note chord, with each note spaced a 3rd apart. The notes can be **blocked** (played at the same time, like a chord) or **broken** (played one at a time, like an arpeggio). To identify a triad, look for the intervals between the notes, to make sure they are all 3rds.

Blocked Triads (Chords)                    Broken Triads (Arpeggios)

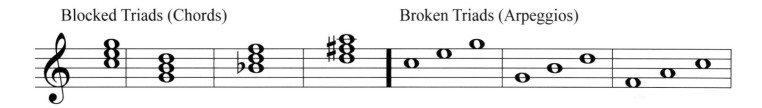

1. Do these notes form a triad? Answer <u>yes</u> or <u>no</u> on each line below, following the example shown.

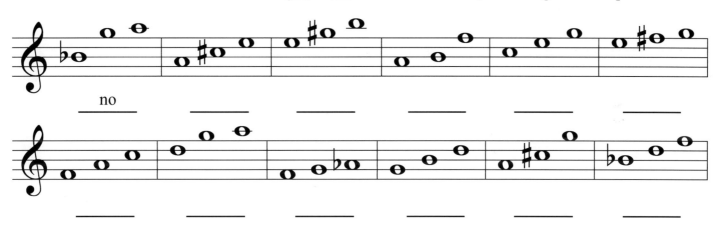

2. Write 2 notes in each measure to form a broken triad (an arpeggio), following the example shown. Do not use accidentals in your answers.

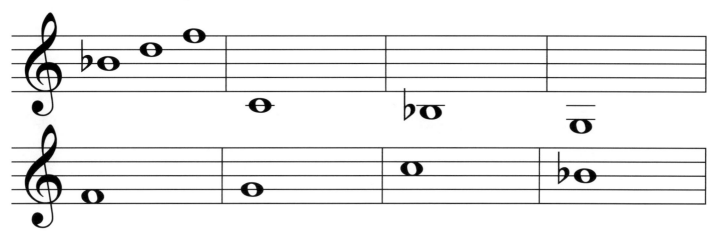

# UNIT 3 REVIEW

## Rhythm

Top number of a time signature:  How many beats are in a measure

Bottom number of a time signature:  The kind of note that gets one beat

The whole rest is held for one measure.  Its length changes with the time signature.

⌢  Fermata:  Hold longer

*rit.*  Ritardando or ritard:  Gradually slower

*a tempo*  Return to the previous speed

## Intervals

Interval:  The distance between two notes

2nd (Step):  Notes on the staff that move from line to space or space to line

3rd (Skip):  Notes on the staff that move from line to line or space to space

## Scales

Scale:  A pattern of 8 notes that moves up and down by step

The half steps in a major scale are between the 3rd and 4th notes and the 7th and 8th notes.

## Triads

Chord:  2 or more notes played together

Arpeggio:  A broken chord (the notes are played one at a time)

Triad:  A three-note chord, with each note spaced a 3rd apart

1.  First write in the counts, then add bar lines to the musical example below.

2.  Write 2nd, 3rd, or unison for each interval.    3.  Do these notes form a triad?  Answer yes or no.

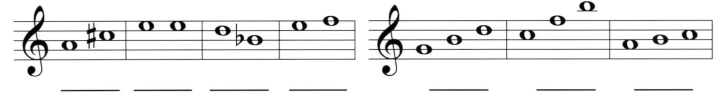

4.  Add half step marks to the notes in the scale below.  Next, circle your answer on the right, to indicate whether or not the scale follows the major scale pattern.

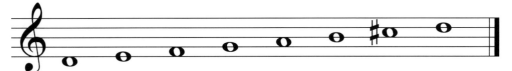

Is this a major scale?
(Circle one:)   Yes   No

# Unit 4

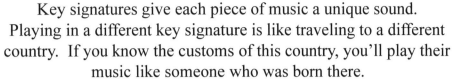

Key signatures give each piece of music a unique sound.
Playing in a different key signature is like traveling to a different
country. If you know the customs of this country, you'll play their
music like someone who was born there.

We'll continue our journey by studying the symbols
and words that appear in music. You'll need to know these
in order to make sense of the road ahead.

Finally, we'll focus on ear training.
This teaches you how to recognize the sounds you hear,
and to play them accurately. Ear training is a skill that
helps you improvise and sightread.

The more you can express yourself through music,
the more fun it is to play!

# Chapter 11
# KEY SIGNATURES

Sharps or flats often appear at the beginning of each line of music, just after the clef. This is called a **key signature**. These sharps or flats apply to all of the notes in the piece. For instance, if there is an F♯ and a C♯ at the beginning of every line, all of the F's and C's in the piece are to be played sharp.

These sharps or flats are called a key signature because they give the music a unique sound, just as each person's signature (the way they sign their name) is the only one of its kind. The sound that each key signature creates is called the **key** or **tonality** of the music.

In the examples below, the F♯ is on the 5th staff line and the C♯ is on the 3rd space. However, the key signature affects every F and C in the music, even the ones that are higher or lower. For example, the low F in measure 4 is also to be played F♯. Only the circled notes in the examples below are sharps or flats, all of the other notes are naturals.

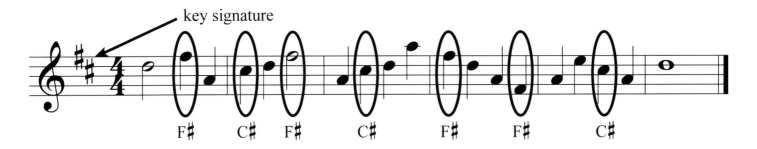

A natural is a note that is *not* sharp or flat. The natural sign can be used to cancel out a sharp or flat in the key signature. Sharps or flats can also be added to the music, to affect notes that are not in the key signature. Compare the musical example below to the one above, to see how the accidentals alter it.

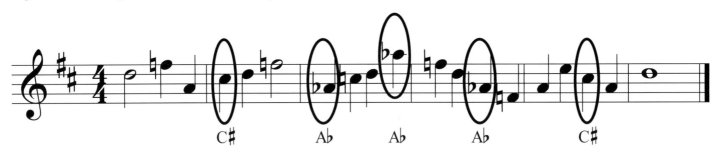

The C, G, and D major scales you learned in Chapter 10 point out which sharps (if any) are used in those keys. Memorize these key signatures.

Key of C Major                    Key of G Major                    Key of D Major

(no sharps or flats)              (1 sharp, F♯)                     (2 sharps, F♯ and C♯)

Circle each of the notes that are to be played sharp or flat in the musical examples below.  Check the key signature and also consider the accidentals.  Write the name of the key in the space provided.

1. Key of _____ Major

2. Key of _____ Major

3. Key of _____ Major

4. Key of _____ Major

5. Key of _____ Major

6. Key of _____ Major

## *Going Beyond*

There is a shortcut to finding the different keys, by using your violin strings!
To find a key with more sharps, go up a 5th.  Remember how the strings are tuned in 5ths?
Start with 3rd finger on the G string to play the note C (the key of C major has no sharps or flats).
Go up a string with 3rd finger to find G, which is the key with 1 sharp.  Go up again and you will find the key with 2 sharps, D Major.  Which key has 3 sharps?  (Hint:  Use your violin strings.)

# Chapter 12
# SIGNS AND TERMS

## Dynamic Markings

Dynamics tell the musician how loud or soft to play. Study the dynamics listed below, which are in order from loudest to softest.

| | | | |
|---|---|---|---|
| *ff* | fortissimo | (for TEE see mo) | very loud |
| *f* | forte | (FOR tay) | loud |
| *mf* | mezzo forte | (MET so for tay) | moderately loud |
| *mp* | mezzo piano | (MET so pee ah no) | moderately soft |
| *p* | piano | (pee AH no) | soft |
| *pp* | pianissimo | (pee ah NEE see mo) | very soft |

The following signs indicate a change in dynamics.

| | | | |
|---|---|---|---|
| ◁ | crescendo (*cresc.*) | (kreh SHEN doh) | gradually louder |
| ▷ | decrescendo (*decresc.*) | (DAY kreh SHEN doh) | gradually softer |
| ▷ | diminuendo (*dim.*) | (dim IN you EN doh) | gradually softer |
| *fp* | fortepiano | (FOR tay pee AH no) | loud, then immediately soft |

## Tempo Markings

| | | | |
|---|---|---|---|
| 𝄐 | fermata | (fur MAH tuh) | hold longer |
| *rit.* | ritard | (rih TARD) | gradually slower |
| *rit.* | ritardando | (rih tar DAHN doh) | gradually slower |
| *a tempo* | a tempo | (AH TEM poh) | return to the previous speed |

## Bowings and Articulations

| | | |
|---|---|---|
| | legato | smooth, connected notes with no pause between them |
| | staccato | short, separate notes; played on the string |
| | accent | play with emphasis |
| | slur | connects two (or more) different notes in one bow |
| | tie | connects two notes of the same pitch; played smoothly |
| | detached slur | a slur with a slight pause between notes |

First memorize all of the signs and terms listed in this chapter. Then answer the following questions, without looking up your answers.

1. When you see *dim.* in the music, play a little bit slower.   True   /   False

2. Write an Italian word that has the same meaning as *decrescendo*. _____

3. **mp** is softer than **mf**.   True   /   False

4. Write the Italian term for "return to the original speed." _____

5. A tie is played smoothly, with no pause between notes.   True   /   False

6. Draw a fermata. ☐

7. An accent is a dynamic marking.   True   /   False

8. *Forte* is pronounced like the word "forty" in English.   True   /   False

9. A slur can connect six notes in one bow.   True   /   False

10. What is the name of the symbol that means hold longer? _____

11. Slurred notes are played legato.   True   /   False

12. A detached slur can connect two notes of the same pitch.   True   /   False

13. To play an accent, make the beginning of the note very strong.   True   /   False

14. Write an Italian word that has the same meaning as *ritardando*. _____

15. **ff** is a dynamic marking.   True   /   False

16. To play staccato, bounce the bow off of the string.   True   /   False

17. Hold a fermata for exactly 3 extra beats.   True   /   False

18. **mp** is softer than **p**.   True   /   False

19. Write the Italian word for this symbol: ◁ _____

20. A detached slur can connect more than two notes in one bow.   True   /   False

21. The marking **fp** means to play loud or play soft.   True   /   False

22. What is the definition of *forte*? _____

23. A tie can connect more than two notes in one bow.   True   /   False

24. The abbreviation *decresc.* stands for the Italian word: _____

25. A *ritard* affects the tempo of a piece.   True   /   False

26. **mf** is softer than **f**.   True   /   False

# Chapter 13
# EAR TRAINING

For each section below, first read the instructions and question, then ask your teacher to play one of the examples. Tell him or her the answer to the question.

Continue to practice these exercises until you can answer accurately every time.

## Scales

Don't watch the music, just listen. Is this a major scale? (Answer <u>yes</u> or <u>no</u>.)

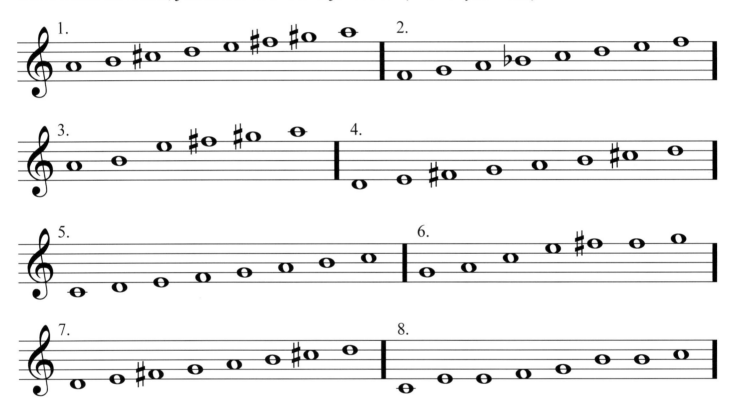

## Triads

Don't watch the music, just listen. Is this a triad? (Answer <u>yes</u> or <u>no</u>.)

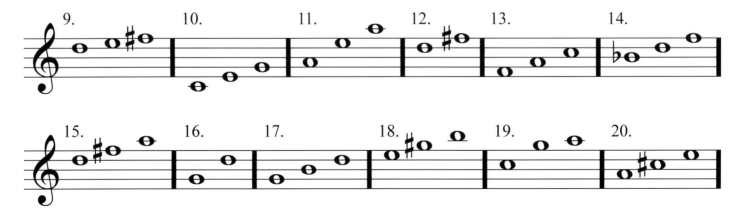

# Articulation

Don't watch the music, just listen.  Do you hear accents or slurs?  (Answer <u>accents</u> or <u>slurs</u>.)

# Rhythm

Watch the music as you listen.  Which rhythm do you hear?  (Answer <u>example a.</u> or <u>example b.</u>)

# FINAL REVIEW

## The Instrument

Finger numbers:  1, 2, 3, 4          Open strings:  E, A, D, G (from highest to lowest)

1st position:  Placing the left hand with 1st finger one note above the open string

◻    Down bow:  Move the bow toward the tip

∨    Up bow:  Move the bow toward the frog

*pizz.*    Pizzicato:  Pluck the string

*arco*    Play with the bow

## The Staff

Staff:  The group of 5 lines and 4 spaces where the music is written

Bar lines:  Lines on the staff that separate the music into small sections

Measure or Bar:  The area between bar lines

‖    Double bar:  The end of the music

:‖    Repeat sign:  Go back and play the music again

1st and 2nd ending:  Play the 1st ending; repeat; skip the 1st ending the second time through

*D.C. al Fine (Da Capo al Fine):*  Return to the beginning, then end at the *Fine*

*D.S. al Fine (Dal Segno al Fine):*  Return to the sign 𝄋, then end at the *Fine*

## Note Values

Note value:  The length of a note; how many counts to hold each note

♬ ꝯ    Sixteenth note & rest:  The note or rest that receives ¼ of a beat (4 in a beat)

♪ 𝄾    Eighth note & rest:  The note or rest that receives ½ of a beat (2 in a beat)

♩ 𝄽    Quarter note & rest:  The note or rest that receives one beat

♩ ▬    Half note & rest:  The note or rest that receives two beats

♩. ▬·    Dotted half note & rest:  The note or rest that receives three beats

𝅝    Whole note:  The note that receives four beats

▬    Whole rest:  The rest that lasts for an entire measure

Notehead:  The main round part of a note

Stem:  The line coming away from a notehead

Lower notes have up stems, and higher notes have down stems

Up stems are on the right side of the notehead, and down stems are on the left side

## Pitch

Pitch:  A term which refers to how high or low a sound is

Musical alphabet:  The 7 letters used to name notes, A B C D E F G

𝄞    Treble clef: The sign at the beginning of each line of music which identifies the note G

Notes on the staff and finger numbers in 1st position:

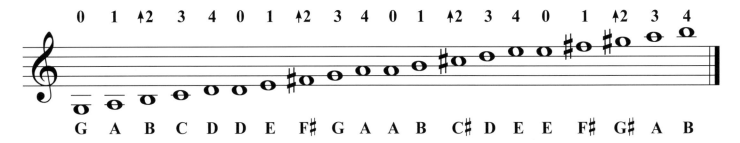

# Accidentals

Half step: The closest distance between two notes

Whole step: The distance of two half steps

Natural note half steps: B to C and E to F are the only natural notes that are a half step apart

♯ Sharp sign: Raises a note by a half step

♭ Flat sign: Lowers a note by a half step

♮ Natural sign: Cancels out a sharp or a flat

# On the Instrument

High 2: 2$^{nd}$ finger is placed close to 3$^{rd}$

Low 2: 2$^{nd}$ finger is placed close to 1$^{st}$

Low 1: 1$^{st}$ finger is placed close to the nut

High 3: 3$^{rd}$ finger is placed close to 4$^{th}$

Legato: Smooth, connected notes with no pause between them

Staccato: Short, separate notes; played on the string

> Accent: Play with emphasis

Slur: Connects two (or more) different notes in one bow

Tie: Connects two notes of the same pitch; held as if the two notes were one

Detached slur: A slur with a slight pause between notes

# Rhythm

Top number of a time signature: How many beats are in a measure

Bottom number of a time signature: The kind of note that gets one beat

𝄐 Fermata: Hold longer

*rit.* Ritardando or ritard: Gradually slower

*a tempo* Return to the previous speed

# Intervals

Interval: The distance between two notes

2$^{nd}$ (Step): Notes on the staff that move from line to space or space to line

3$^{rd}$ (Skip): Notes on the staff that move from line to line or space to space

# Scales and Triads

The half steps in a major scale are between the 3$^{rd}$ and 4$^{th}$ notes and the 7$^{th}$ and 8$^{th}$ notes

Triad: A three-note chord, with each note spaced a 3$^{rd}$ apart

# Key Signatures

Key Signature: The group of sharps or flats to the right of the clef that identifies the key

C Major—no sharps or flats; G Major—1 sharp (F♯); D Major—2 sharps (F♯ and C♯)

# Dynamics

| | | | | |
|---|---|---|---|---|
| ***ff*** | Fortissimo: Very loud | | ***mp*** | Mezzo piano: Moderately soft |
| ***f*** | Forte: Loud | | ***p*** | Piano: Soft |
| ***mf*** | Mezzo forte: Moderately loud | | ***pp*** | Pianissimo: Very soft |

Crescendo (*cresc.*): Gradually louder

Decrescendo (*decresc.*)

Diminuendo (*dim.*): Gradually softer

***fp*** Fortepiano: Loud, then immediately soft

# Special Assignment

Writing your own music is called **composition**.

Music is often written in small sections, called "question and answer" or "call and response." The sections can be labeled A, B, A, and B[1]. The A section feels incomplete, like it's asking a question. Then the B section responds to that question. B doesn't feel quite like the end of the piece, but the B[1] section finally resolves by ending on the note that names the key. Play "Mary Had a Little Lamb" on your violin, noticing the differences between the marked sections.

**Mary Had a Little Lamb**

Follow the steps below to compose your own piece of music. Check that you've followed the steps carefully. Finally, show this to your teacher.

1.  Play the A section (below) on your violin.
2.  Think of two measures that could follow it, ending on any note except D.
3.  Write these notes in measures 3 and 4. Play the first line on your violin.
4.  If you want to change any of the notes, you can do that, then play the measures again.
5.  Write a treble clef and the D Major key signature on the second line.
6.  Copy all of the notes from the first A section into measures 5 and 6.
7.  Think of two measures that start like the B section on the 1st line, but end on the note D.
8.  Write these notes in measures 7 and 8. Finish it with a double bar.
9.  Check that each measure has the correct number of beats.
10. Give your composition a title. Write it above the staff.
11. Bring it to life. Play it!

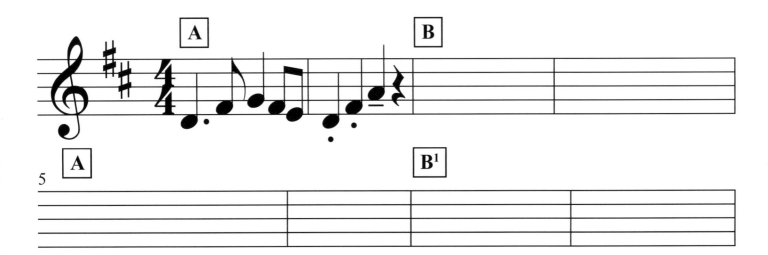

# Congratulations!

You've now made it through
all of the lessons in the workbook.

Take some time to review the book.
Focus on topics you didn't understand and
questions you answered incorrectly.

You've done a great job!

# Practice Tests

You've worked hard
to get through all of these lessons.
Now let's make sure you understand and remember it all!
The following practice tests will help you do that.

Do one practice test at a time.
Don't forget to use a pencil.  No pens allowed!
Make sure it's fully corrected and that you understand
any questions you answered incorrectly before moving on
to the next test.  This will give you confidence
that you know the material well, and
are ready for the next level.

Stick with your study of music theory
and you will see the benefits:  the music you play
will make more sense, and this will lead to a
lifelong enjoyment of music.

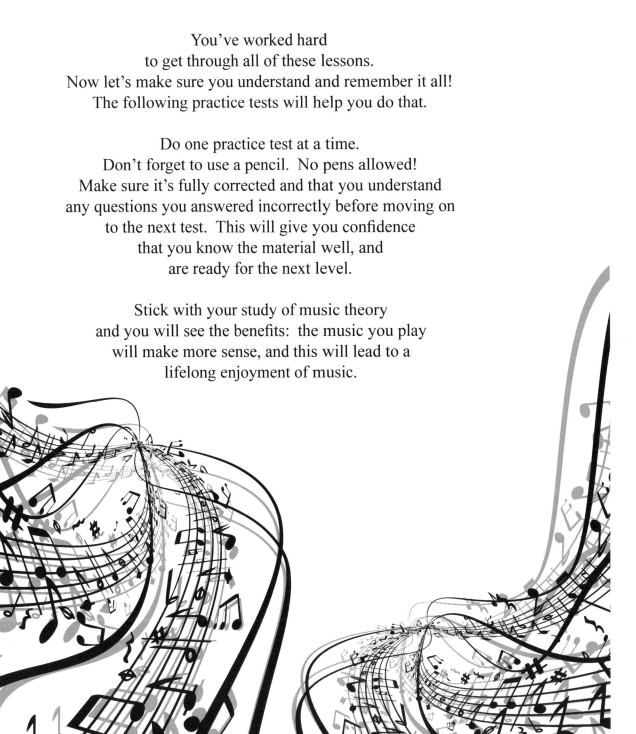

# Chapter 14
## PRACTICE TEST 1

1. Do these notes form a triad?  Answer <u>yes</u> or <u>no</u> on each line below.

___  ___  ___  ___  ___  ___

2. Write the finger number and the note name for each note in 1<sup>st</sup> position, following the example shown.  Use arrows to indicate low 1, low 2, high 2, and high 3.

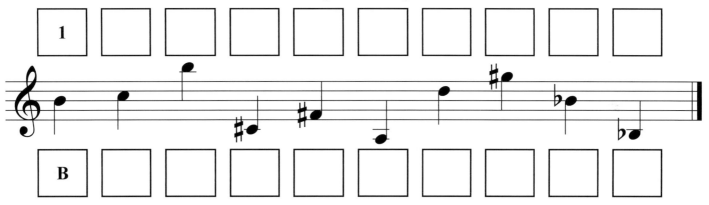

3. Write a major scale on the staff below, starting on the printed note.  If sharps or flats are needed, use accidentals, not a key signature.

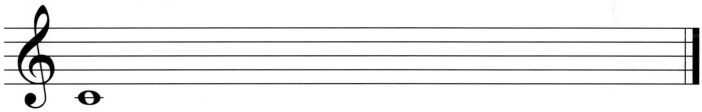

4. Write <u>2nd</u>, <u>3rd</u>, or <u>unison</u> under each measure.

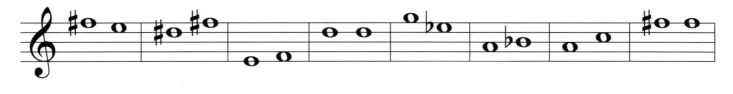

___  ___  ___  ___  ___  ___

5. Mark all of the half steps on the musical example below, following the example shown.

6. Add bar lines to the musical example below.  Finish with a double bar.

7. Complete the line of music by writing one <u>REST</u> below each arrow.

8. Write <u>H</u> for half step or <u>W</u> for whole step below.

9. Identify the notes and rests on the staff below, following the example shown.

10. Circle each of the notes that are to be played sharp or flat in the musical example below.  Then write the name of the key in the space provided.

Key of _____ Major

11. Write <u>S for slur</u>, <u>T for tie</u>, or <u>D for detached slur</u> below each measure.

Refer to the piece below as you answer questions 12 to 24.

12. What is the name of the articulation used in measures 5 to 7? _____

13. What is the correct order of performance for this piece? (Check one.)

_____ a. measure 1-8, 4-8
_____ b. measure 1-4, 7-8, 1-4
_____ c. measure 1-8, 1-4

14. What are the lines above the note in measure 8 called? _____

15. What is the name of the musical symbol over the note in measure 4? _____

16. Does the first accidental in measure 2 affect any other notes in that measure? _____

17. Should measure 4 be played faster or slower than Andante? _____

18. Write the Italian word(s) for the dynamic marking in measure 5. _____

19. What is the boxed interval in measure 2? (Circle one:)   2nd   /   3rd

20. How many beats are in measure 8? _____

21. How many times does the note E♭ appear on the first line of this piece? _____

22. What does the marking under measure 3 mean? _____

23. What is the name of the boxed rest in measure 8? _____

24. In the performance of this piece, how many times will a slur be played? _____

# Practice Test 1: Ear Training

**Stop here.** Take this to your teacher in order to complete the test.

<u>Instructions for the teacher:</u>
The student should not look at the music for this portion of the test. First, read the question to the student. Then, play the example slowly, and mark the student's answer. Play it repeatedly if he/she is unsure of the answer. For the last two lines, ask the student to watch the music as you play.

Ask the student: "Is this a major scale? Answer <u>yes</u> or <u>no</u>."

25. ☐ Yes  ☐ No

26. ☐ Yes  ☐ No

Ask the student: "Is this a triad? Answer <u>yes</u> or <u>no</u>."

27. ☐ Yes  ☐ No

28. ☐ Yes  ☐ No

Ask the student: "Do you hear accents or slurs? Answer <u>accents</u> or <u>slurs</u>."

29. ☐ Accents  ☐ Slurs

30. ☐ Accents  ☐ Slurs

Have the student watch the music while listening, as the teacher plays one of the lines below.

31. Which rhythm do you hear? (Check one.)

☐

☐

# Grading

Perfect Score: 124 points    Number Incorrect: _____

Perfect Score - Number Incorrect = Final Score: _____

Final Score divided by 124 = Percentage: _____

# Chapter 15
# PRACTICE TEST 2

1. Identify the notes and rests on the staff below, following the example shown.

half ____ ____ ____ ____ ____ ____ ____ ____

note ____ ____ ____ ____ ____ ____ ____ ____

2. Circle each of the notes that are to be played sharp or flat in the musical example below. Then write the name of the key in the space provided.

Key of _____ Major

3. Mark all of the half steps on the musical example below, following the example shown.

4. Write <u>2nd</u>, <u>3rd</u>, or <u>unison</u> under each measure.

____ ____ ____ ____ ____ ____ ____

5. Write a major scale on the staff below, starting on the printed note. If sharps or flats are needed, use accidentals, not a key signature.

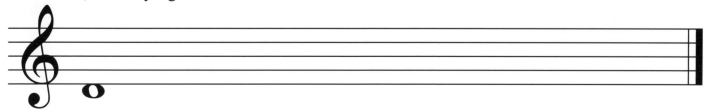

6. Write <u>S for slur</u>, <u>T for tie</u>, or <u>D for detached slur</u> below each measure.

_____

7. Write the finger number and the note name for each note in 1<sup>st</sup> position, following the example shown. Use arrows to indicate low 1, low 2, high 2, and high 3.

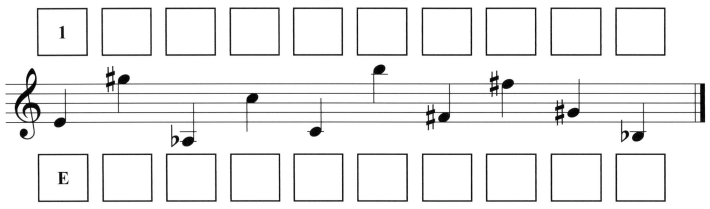

8. Write <u>H</u> for half step or <u>W</u> for whole step below.

_____

9. Do these notes form a triad? Answer <u>yes</u> or <u>no</u> on each line below.

_____

10. Add bar lines to the musical example below. Finish with a double bar.

11. Complete the line of music by writing one <u>REST</u> below each arrow.

Refer to the piece below as you answer questions 12 to 24.

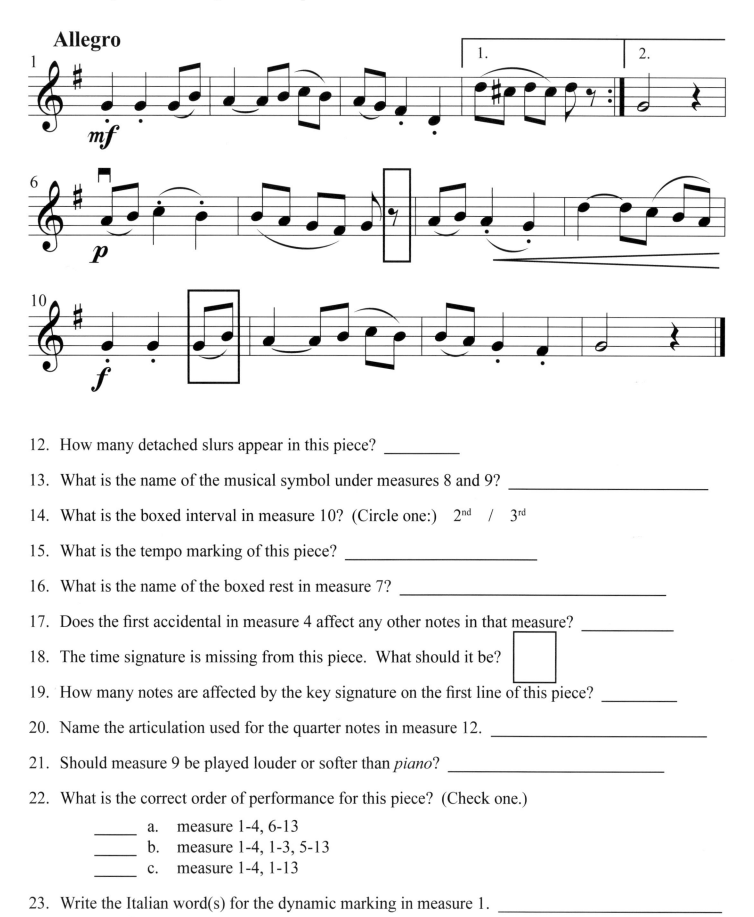

12. How many detached slurs appear in this piece? _____

13. What is the name of the musical symbol under measures 8 and 9? _____

14. What is the boxed interval in measure 10? (Circle one:)   2nd   /   3rd

15. What is the tempo marking of this piece? _____

16. What is the name of the boxed rest in measure 7? _____

17. Does the first accidental in measure 4 affect any other notes in that measure? _____

18. The time signature is missing from this piece. What should it be?

19. How many notes are affected by the key signature on the first line of this piece? _____

20. Name the articulation used for the quarter notes in measure 12. _____

21. Should measure 9 be played louder or softer than *piano*? _____

22. What is the correct order of performance for this piece? (Check one.)

    _____ a.  measure 1-4, 6-13
    _____ b.  measure 1-4, 1-3, 5-13
    _____ c.  measure 1-4, 1-13

23. Write the Italian word(s) for the dynamic marking in measure 1. _____

24. In the performance of this piece, how many times will a tie be played? _____

# Practice Test 2:  Ear Training

**Stop here.**  Take this to your teacher in order to complete the test.

Instructions for the teacher:
The student should not look at the music for this portion of the test.  First, read the question to the student.  Then, play the example slowly, and mark the student's answer.  Play it repeatedly if he/she is unsure of the answer.  For the last two lines, ask the student to watch the music as you play.

Ask the student: "Is this a major scale?  Answer <u>yes</u> or <u>no</u>."

25. ☐ Yes
    ☐ No

26. ☐ Yes
    ☐ No

Ask the student: "Is this a triad?  Answer <u>yes</u> or <u>no</u>."

27. ☐ Yes
    ☐ No

28. ☐ Yes
    ☐ No

Ask the student: "Do you hear accents or slurs?  Answer <u>accents</u> or <u>slurs</u>."

29. ☐ Accents
    ☐ Slurs

30. ☐ Accents
    ☐ Slurs

Have the student watch the music while listening, as the teacher plays one of the lines below.

31. Which rhythm do you hear?  (Check one.)

☐

☐

## Grading

Perfect Score:  120 points      Number Incorrect: _____

Perfect Score - Number Incorrect = Final Score: _____

Final Score divided by 120 = Percentage: _____

# Chapter 16
# PRACTICE TEST 3

1. Write <u>S for slur</u>, <u>T for tie</u>, or <u>D for detached slur</u> below each measure.

2. Write <u>H</u> for half step or <u>W</u> for whole step below.

3. Complete the line of music by writing one <u>REST</u> below each arrow.

4. Mark all of the half steps on the musical example below, following the example shown.

5. Write <u>2nd</u>, <u>3rd</u>, or <u>unison</u> under each measure.

6. Add bar lines to the musical example below. Finish with a double bar.

7. Identify the notes and rests on the staff below, following the example shown.

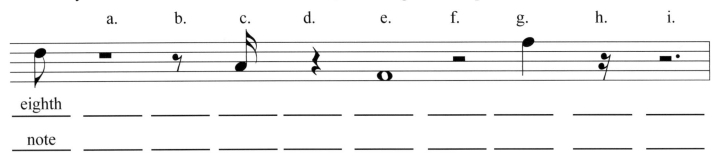

eighth _____ _____ _____ _____ _____ _____ _____ _____

note _____ _____ _____ _____ _____ _____ _____ _____

8. Write the finger number and the note name for each note in 1st position, following the example shown. Use arrows to indicate low 1, low 2, high 2, and high 3.

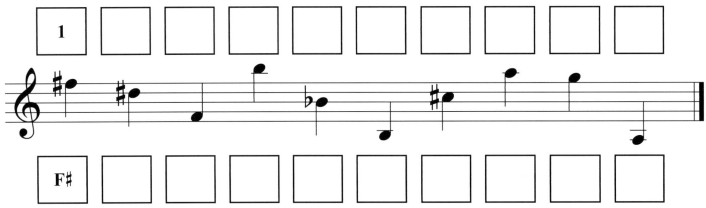

9. Circle each of the notes that are to be played sharp or flat in the musical example below. Then write the name of the key in the space provided.

Key of _____ Major

10. Write a major scale on the staff below, starting on the printed note. If sharps or flats are needed, use accidentals, not a key signature.

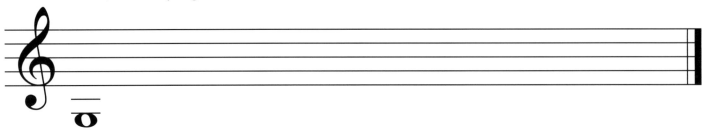

11. Do these notes form a triad? Answer yes or no on each line below.

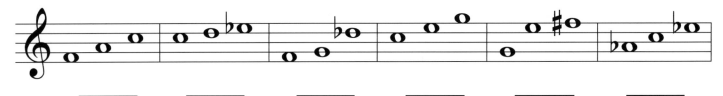

Refer to the piece below as you answer questions 12 to 24.

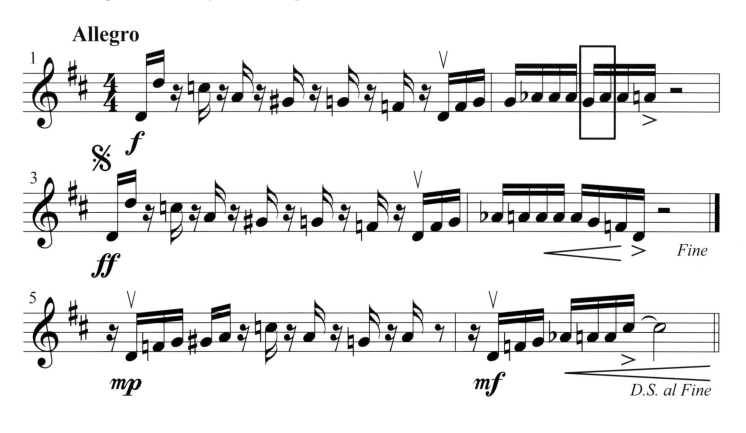

12. How many sixteenth notes are written in the 1ˢᵗ measure? _____

13. What is the name of the articulation used in measure 4? _____

14. What is the boxed interval in measure 2? (Circle one:)   Half step   /   Whole step

15. What is the tempo marking of this piece? _____

16. Which is the loudest measure? _____

17. Does the first accidental in measure 3 affect any other notes in that measure? _____

18. In which two measures does the music gradually change in volume? _____ and _____

19. How many notes are affected by the key signature on the 3ʳᵈ line of this piece? _____

20. Do the first 3 notes in measure 5 form a triad? _____

21. What does the word *Fine* in measure 4 mean in English? _____

22. What is the correct order of performance for this piece?  (Check one.)

    _____ a.   measure 1-6, 3-4
    _____ b.   measure 1-6, 1-4
    _____ c.   measure 1-4, 3-6

23. Write the Italian word(s) for the dynamic marking in measure 5. _____

24. In the performance of this piece, how many times will a tie be played? _____

# Practice Test 3:  Ear Training

**Stop here.**  Take this to your teacher in order to complete the test.

<u>Instructions for the teacher:</u>
The student should not look at the music for this portion of the test.  First, read the question to the student.  Then, play the example slowly, and mark the student's answer.  Play it repeatedly if he/she is unsure of the answer.  For the last two lines, ask the student to watch the music as you play.

Ask the student:  "Is this a major scale?  Answer <u>yes</u> or <u>no</u>."

25. ☐ Yes    ☐ No

26. ☐ Yes    ☐ No

Ask the student:  "Is this a triad?  Answer <u>yes</u> or <u>no</u>."

27. ☐ Yes    ☐ No

28. ☐ Yes    ☐ No

Ask the student:  "Do you hear accents or slurs?  Answer <u>accents</u> or <u>slurs</u>."

29. ☐ Accents    ☐ Slurs

30. ☐ Accents    ☐ Slurs

Have the student watch the music while listening, as the teacher plays one of the lines below.

31. Which rhythm do you hear?  (Check one.)

☐

☐

## Grading

# INDEX

# Core Music Theory for String Players

### *An essential resource for string students*

**ORDER ONLINE**
**www.coremusictheory.com**

- Violin Preparatory Level
  - Violin Level 1
    - Violin Level 2
      - Violin Level 3
        - Violin Level 4
          - Violin Level 5
            - Violin Level 6
              - Violin Level 7
                - Violin Level 8
                  - Violin Level 9
                    - Violin Level 10
                      - Violin Answer Key

- Viola Preparatory Level
  - Viola Level 1
    - Viola Level 2
      - Viola Level 3
        - Viola Level 4
          - Viola Level 5
            - Viola Level 6
              - Viola Level 7
                - Viola Level 8
                  - Viola Level 9
                    - Viola Level 10
                      - Viola Answer Key

- Cello Preparatory Level
  - Cello Level 1
    - Cello Level 2
      - Cello Level 3
        - Cello Level 4
          - Cello Level 5
            - Cello Level 6
              - Cello Level 7
                - Cello Level 8
                  - Cello Level 9
                    - Cello Level 10
                      - Cello Answer Key

- Bass Preparatory Level
  - Bass Level 1
    - Bass Level 2
      - Bass Level 3
        - Bass Level 4
          - Bass Level 5
            - Bass Level 6
              - Bass Level 7
                - Bass Level 8
                  - Bass Level 9
                    - Bass Level 10
                      - Bass Answer Key